LIZ JENNINGS

Blank for Your Own Message

A Collection of Short Stories about Parents and Children

Copyright © 2019 Liz Jennings
All rights reserved.

ISBN: 1-9997464-7-3
ISBN-13: 978-1-9997464-7-6

For all the parents and children I have known, with thanks

Blank for Your Own Message

CONTENTS

1. Chances Are 1
2. Dream House 13
3. Dolores, Cosmo and Stanley 19
4. Hair 29
5. Finders, Keepers 31
6. Play Date 43
7. What A Way To Go 51
8. Working From Home 63
9. Starting Small 71
10. The Easy Option 77
11. Fish On Holiday 87
12. Something To Do 91
About the Author 97

Blank for Your Own Message

Chances Are

IT WAS AFTER Daniel did badly in his SATs that I hit upon the idea.

I'd gone fishing while he was at school. I go to the pier. I don't mind the snag risk for my line, you just get used to it. And, since I was made redundant, I've had more opportunity than most to get used to it.

I always head right down to the north corner, looking across towards Dunkirk, not that I look up very often: my eyes are fixed on the waves. There's always a lot of guys fishing, hoping and waiting for a gift from below.

I stood there that day, listening to the water moving, feeling the wind freezing the drip on the tip of my nose, hearing the groan of the timbers protesting pointlessly against the waves, and I thought about how, for six and a half years, my son had let me down again and again and again.

I'd watched him falling over in places without any apparent obstacles, tripping up on invisible hazards. He'd constantly failed to recognise his own name at the pre-school, where it was printed clearly on a paper leaf - all he had to do was stick it on a cardboard tree. He'd held story books upside-down and back-to-front more times than I could count. He put his shoes on the wrong feet and his hands in the wrong gloves. He pulled the sleeves of his fleece inside out when he took it off, and then couldn't put it back on again because he forgot what he did and the fleece no longer made sense to him when he came back to it. He spilt drinks daily and occasionally blew raspberries at complete strangers. He had said 'Bum' to the dentist when she'd asked him to open wide, and he sometimes scribbled on other children's colouring.

Any time he's asked to look after anything, he's guaranteed to lose it. Anything he orders in a café, he doesn't want when it arrives. He still wets the bed three nights out of seven. He can't button his own shirt up or tie his laces. His writing is scrawly and his reading is painfully slow.

Every mistake he makes reminds me of those glory days before he was born. I'd lay my cheek on Georgina's rounded belly and coo at our little miracle. He'd wiggle and jiggle inside there, and I'd gently press my hands on her tight skin, playing guess-the-body part.

I fantasized about the things I'd do with my wonderful child - mostly fishing, I admit. I pictured us going home to Georgina with tales of the ones that got away, the occasional triumphant trophy - always a mackerel in my daydreams. In my silly fantasies we'd cook it up, and the three of us would eat and laugh, like something out of an advert.

I thought about that daydream, and smiled sourly, as I reeled my line in. The bait was gone; the cold hook naked but for a dripping slink of deep green seaweed. I skewered another limp flash of dead fish onto its point, and cast out again.

Back then, with Georgina lying there smiling at my hand on her beautiful belly, there was only hope. The intense, terrifying hope that comes before everything changes forever. This little person was going to complete the puzzle.

But our puzzle will never be completed, because Georgina died. You don't hear very often of mothers dying in childbirth these days. I thought it was something that happened in Victorian Britain or maybe modern day Africa. I had been so confident in the simple equation of *mummy plus daddy equals baby*. But in the end which marked a beginning, Georgina died so that Daniel could live.

And suddenly here we were, alone together. My world all caved in, his just opening up. I ate toast three times a day, and left work to care for my wife's killer. I stood like an angry linesman at toddler groups, staring hard at the kids who snatched, shaking my head in warning at mischief makers and flinching at every mention of *mummy*.

As the months went on, my despair spread across the surface of my life. Where had all that hope gone? All that anticipated joy… where was it? Again and again, Daniel let me down.

I'd brought Daniel fishing, just once. I'd dug my old rod out from the pile of stuff I didn't want to deal with in the loft. It was a beautiful deep green, a present from my Grandad when I was eight years old. I tried to make Daniel understand how special this rod was, but he was too excited to take anything in, hopping about like an idiot, whistling. He does that when he's overexcited. Stands there whistling. Like his mouth can't form words.

We'd been here on the north corner of the pier for about three minutes when Daniel let go of my rod. We watched in silence as it dropped the fifteen feet or so from the pier railing to the sea, and bobbed out on the water thanks to its cork handle, drifting off towards Dunkirk.

I hadn't said a word, just packed up the rest of our kit and started back down the pier, with Daniel jogging to keep up. We'd gone home, not in triumph, but in silence. Then he'd started crying, and I'd started shouting. My volume finally drowned his out, and by the time I'd pushed him through the door into the flat, he was silently swallowing sobs, making dribble from the corners of his mouth.

I've not brought him fishing again.

Disappointment filled me like a bad smell. My son was a failure.

And so it was that my idea began to form. I needed some hope for the future. I couldn't face a life of disappointment like this. I telephoned a number of insurance companies, but the woman I spoke to on my fifth call… well, she changed everything.

"I'd like to insure against my child disappointing me," I said.

"I beg your pardon, sir?"

"I want to insure against disappointment; can you do that?" I sighed, bored by the number of times I'd repeated this question already today.

"What sort of disappointment?" Her voice was low, slightly husky, like she was recovering from a cold.

"Oh, you know, failed exam results, picking bad girlfriends, becoming a Goth - that sort of thing."

"Who are you talking about, sir?"

"Pardon?"

"Who do you think may be likely to disappoint you?"

"My son."

"Your son?"

"Look, are you able to give me a quote or not?"

"This is a very unusual request sir,"

"I can't think why."

"Might I suggest, sir, that you may be better off going to a bookmaker and placing a bet that your son will certainly disappoint you, probably repeatedly?"

"I'm sorry?"

All the other companies had turned my request down by now. Was she being sarcastic, or was that a genuine suggestion?

"It's just that it's fairly inevitable, isn't it?"

"What is?"

"Disappointment. Pardon me for getting rather philosophical, sir, but to live is surely to face the daily possibility of being disappointed. Have you considered the thought that maybe you're expecting too much?"

"How do you know what I'm expecting?" She was rubbing me up the wrong way, this one.

"Well, obviously, I don't."

Ha! Gotcha!

"No, I didn't think you did. I expected my wife to live. That's why the life insurance was some compensation when she died."

"Was it? Really?"

Damn.

"No."

"I'm sorry you lost your wife sir."

"Thank you."

"That must have been very difficult for you."

"I've had enough of sadness - I need this insurance policy."

"You *need* it?"

"I need something to hope for again."

"But you'd be hoping for disappointment, sir."

"Not necessarily," I countered, but her silence left me floundering. "I mean, is it unreasonable to expect someone to grasp the basic rules of addition and subtraction?"

"All kids do, eventually, don't they, sir?"

"Not if they're dyscalculiate, they don't. Or what if he turns out to be plain lazy? Or not very bright? Or what if he doesn't make friends? Or takes up smoking? Or starts doing drugs? What if he drops out of school? Or worse, gets kicked out?"

"Do you feel that perhaps you're not giving him a chance?"

"I've given him chances every day since he was born. And every day, in pretty much every way, he's let me down."

"Then, forgive me sir, but it might not be in our interests for us to allow such a policy: we'd be making daily pay-outs."

"I'd pay the premiums. It'd give me something to look forward to."

"But humans make mistakes, sir. Unless your son is a robot or a gingerbread man, he will make mistakes. That's just life."

"Listen, the gingerbread man made a fatal mistake, trusting that fox. If his parents had been able to insure against that, it might have provided some comfort at what must have been a very difficult time for them."

"Enough money to buy some new flour and butter, you mean, sir? "

"Don't be facetious. I can hear you laughing, you know. What I'm saying is that I understand that life is full of twists and turns, but I don't want it to be. So I'd like to take out a policy please. The simple question is, will you or won't you help me?"

"Well, sir, I think we can help you."

"Good. About time." I smiled, but I didn't feel happy.

"But you need to understand that an insurance policy is a contract. If we make a policy for you insuring *you* against being disappointed by your son, we will have to make a contractually balanced policy for your son, should he wish to make a counter-claim."

"Counter claim?"

"Yes sir. Insurance is a two-way street."

"A two-way street?" I heard myself repeating idiotically.

"That's right. We'd need to speak to your son about a policy of his own."

"And what, exactly, would his policy contain?"

"Well, it would be in relation to your disappointing him, sir. "

"Me?"

"Yes, sir'"

"In what way can you possibly mean?"

"Well, for example, there may be times when you fail to provide him with a nutritionally balanced diet."

"I beg your pardon?"

"And you may not dress him warmly enough for cold weather, so he might be out and feel a bit chilly. That would be disappointing for him, don't you think?" Her voice was getting a little bit louder with each word.

"Eh?"

"Or you might forget when it's non-uniform day and send him to school in the wrong clothes; you might not give him the present he really wanted for his birthday or you might take him on holiday to somewhere he doesn't like. Or perhaps you'll simply fail to show, say... unconditional love, maybe, I don't know. But, suffice to say, something like that would be very disappointing for a child. Harmful, even."

Her voice had grown so loud that the silence that followed her words was shocking, like peace after gunfire. Finally, I found some words of my own, but they rang in my ears, strained and artificially high in pitch, and I made myself think of the word *pompous*.

"Are you insinuating-?"

"Sir, I wouldn't dream of it. I'm simply pointing out the possibilities of the equal and opposite insurance policy we'd need to draw up in order to create an environment where your claims against your son would be valid."

I pressed the red button on my phone handset, and ended the call. I yanked my coat from its hook by the door and headed out to the car, opened the boot: my fishing stuff was all there; I knew it was there, but it made me feel better just seeing it. The rancid stench of dried-up bait hit me like a cherished lover with bad breath.

I shut the boot and went back into the house. I paced the hallway a few times, put the kettle on, turned it off again, poured myself a glass of water from the tap, and headed back to the lounge. Perhaps I would phone that woman back.

I pulled the curtains back a little, and stared out of the window. A man in his fifties pushed an elderly man in a wheelchair. The man in the wheelchair reached his hand back over his shoulder and patted the fingers of the younger man, grasped them and held on. The old man had drool on his chin that caught the sunlight and sparkled for a moment.

I turned away.

The number for the school was written on a scrap of paper that was pinned by a magnet to the fridge door. I spoke to the secretary, who sounded like she was in her usual foul mood, and let her know that I would be coming to collect Daniel early today for a dental appointment.

She tutted. "What time is your appointment?"

"Two thirty," I said, smiling at how you never forget the jokes you learn as a child. She didn't even pick up on it. At two o'clock I walked into the school reception to find Daniel looking anxious.

"Hello, Daniel."

"What's wrong?"

"Nothing's wrong, mate."

The word *mate* felt unnatural in my mouth, I didn't seem able to say it without sounding faintly threatening. "Come on, then," I reached out my hand.

"Where are we going?"

I felt the secretary's eye on us, suspicious, irritated.

"To the dentist's, of course," I winked at Daniel. Winking didn't suit me, I could feel it. It looked more like a nervous tic than a secret message of fun to be had.

Outside the school, I opened the car door wide.

"We usually walk to the dentist's," he said. He looked uncertain, anxious, as if he'd be glad to be called back into the school.

"Get in, Daniel," I said. I shut his door, and strode around the front of the car, pulled at my door handle a little too eagerly, lost my grip on it, pulled again, more gently this time, and hauled myself into the driving seat.

Daniel looked confused, tearful even. "I'm sorry, Dad, whatever I did, I don't mean to-"

I leaned across the gear stick and pulled his head to my chest. "No. Not you. *Me*. I'm sorry, Daniel."

"Dad?" He looked up at me, uncertain in this unknown territory. His sad eyes glistened. Mine did, too.

"We're going out, Daniel."

"Where to?"

He pressed back into his seat, like maybe he didn't even want to be here at all. I felt my bravado waver, like a fool on a first date, reading all the signals wrong after too many bathroom-mirror rehearsals.

"Where would you like to go? We can do whatever you'd like to do. McDonalds, the fair, the toyshop - you name it."

"What do *you* want to do, Dad?"

"Me?"

"I don't mind what I do."

I had to look away. I'd suddenly seen the child, so desperate to please his unpleasable father, searching for the right answer, looking for a destination without a map. And then I realise for the first time that he has Georgina's way of holding his hands, fingers knotted together in a twisted puzzle. I suddenly remembered her whistling: why hadn't I remembered that before?

"Son, it's not about me," I say. "You choose."

"But you might not like my choice."

"You choose."

There's a silence between us. Another car drives past: an old woman on a zimmer frame passes with a small, black wiry-haired dog that yaps at us until the woman has to drag it away by its cow-print patterned lead. And all the time, Daniel is staring at me, and I'm staring at him, and stealing glances at the dog, and staring back at Daniel, and glancing at the dog, and the woman, and the cow-print patterned lead, and then he smiles. And I see it in his eyes: uncertainty and hope, in equal measure. And I know, I just *know,* right then, I know exactly what he wants to do. And I'm glad, because, for once in my life, I'm ready.

Dream House

IT'S SEVEN O'CLOCK on the last evening of half term when Harry first tells me about his homework. He stands on the cold kitchen tiles in his Disney pyjamas looking thoroughly relaxed, fiddling with a half-finished loom band that he's found buried down between the sofa cushions.

"You've got to make a complete model of your dream house *by tomorrow*?" I say, squeezing a teabag with my bare fingers, the pain of the wet burn stinging in a pleasantly distracting way.

"From recycling,' he says, and I can hear in his voice he thinks he's actually being helpful by elaborating.

"From the recycling that the bin men took away on Friday morning, do you mean?" I indicate the empty green tub in our kitchen.

"Well we can make some more recycling."

"I know where there's some." His sister drops the slime she's pulling at onto the worktop and runs from the kitchen. She's been pinching sweets again while I wasn't looking. There's a brown chocolate ring around her mouth and chin.

"You need your face wiped!" I shout to an empty hallway as the downstairs toilet door closes behind her.

"I could eat a whole box of Cheerios," Harry says, thinking he's being helpful again.

"I'll see what I can find," I say, opening a cupboard and rummaging through the shelves. There's some icing sugar that's almost finished. I rip the inner packet from the cardboard outside, a cloud of fine white powder shooting upwards and settling on the front of my navy jumper.

"That's brilliant, Mummy," Harry says, trying toencourage me. I sigh and brush my hands over my chest, rubbing the sugar deeper into the wool.

I remember a shoebox upstairs. "Hang on," I say, my mood surprising me, swinging unexpectedly to one of excitement, "I've got something that might just be brilliant."

Harry jumps up and down, and it does lift my spirits to see him excited and to know that I'm about to make his day.

The toilet door is closed as I pass.

"What are you doing in there, Nancy?"

No answer comes, and I move on.

The kitchen table looks like a scene from Blue Peter: a shoebox, empty sugar packet, roll of sticky tape, scissors and felt tip pens.

"I know exactly what I'm going to do," Harry grins.

"Well, that sounds like you don't need any help from me," I say, sensing a coffee and a quick phone call to see how my Mum is.

Nancy appears with an empty toilet roll. "This'll be good," she smiles.

I look at the roll, then walk down the hall and slowly pull the toilet door open: the room is covered in the toilet paper that's been unwound and discarded to provide the roll for her brother.

"Nancy," I say, wrapping the yards and yards of tissue around my hand. I hear Nancy run out of the back door.

The first day back after half term, and thirty parents make their ways to school in the wind and rain, protecting their children's dream houses like pink, bald puppies in their arms.

Harry insists on carrying his own in.

I think he's done well. He's stuck the sugar packet in the middle of the shoebox, and made the top flaps meet to form a triangle for a roof. He's found some cotton wool and stuck it to the roof to create the effect of smoke coming from a non-existent chimney. He's drawn windows and a door over the writing on the sugar packet.

The loo roll has been unfurled and stuck to the shoebox behind the sugar-packet-house: it's a race track, which would be in the back garden of Harry's dream home. Not bad, for a five year old, I think to myself. Initiative and invention. He'll probably become an engineer and create something awesome that I can keep newspaper cuttings about and show my hairdresser, or pharmacist, one day.

Harry hands his creation to me to take care of while he hangs his coat up. I'm getting a bit twitchy, because I only have ten minutes to get Nancy into pre-school. His dream house is a bit front heavy, and I nearly drop it.

"Careful, Mummy," Harry says, worried. He reaches for his model and takes it back from me, cradling it protectively.

"Is it alright, Harry?" Nancy asks, almost whispering to her brother, her eyes flicking to me for a moment with the merest frown, as if I were some cack-handed fool who nearly ruined everything they've worked towards.

As we head for Harry's classroom, past all the coats and bags piled onto pegs, we meet Troy. I know all about Troy because he's constantly getting Red Cards for bad behaviour. The only thing Harry ever tells me about what actually happens for six hours a day in this building is who got given a red card and who got sent to see the headmaster because they were in trouble.

We all see Troy's dream house at the same moment. We can't miss it, because Troy is holding it out in front of him as if it were Cinderella's slipper and he is the Royal Page.

It looks like Hogwarts: there are turrets, and spires and ramparts; there's a moat partially filled with what looks like water but is set solid. *There are fish in the moat.*

"How did you-?"

I bend down to look more closely. There are lights on inside the castle, shining through little plastic see-through windows. There's fake grass and ducks and even a weathercock attached to the top of the tallest turret.

Troy's mother bends over Harry's sugar packet.

"Aww, well done little fella, that's lovely," she says. I look at my shoes: I cannot bear to see her expression.

"Thanks," Harry beams. "Yours is epic, Troy."

"Yes," I say, "That must've taken hours and hours and hours. Did you leave the house at all during half term?"

"Oh, we've been at Disney Paris all week," Troy's mother says, pushing her thick blonde hair behind her ear, "It's been brilliant, hasn't it Troy?" She ruffles his hair. "I think that's what inspired Troy with his dream house."

"Lovely," I say. "Good work, Troy. Fancy doing that all by yourself! Well, come on then, Harry, let's get you into your classroom," I say, pushing Harry in the back and dragging Nancy by the hand. Nancy passes Troy's model, wide-eyed and open-mouthed.

The classroom is full of dream houses. It seems this half term's task really captured the imaginations of the group. There are chocolate factories, toy factories, miniature versions of Downton Abbey, soft play centres just ten inches high complete with slides and coloured rollers to squeeze between. There are bakeries and caves, treasure islands surrounded by realistic oceans filled with jumping dolphins and the tails of breaching whales. It looks like a model village in here.

"Honestly, Harry, I wish you'd given me a bit a more notice about this," I say.

I place Harry's sugar packet at the back, on the end, behind a foot-high lighthouse, painted in red and white stripes with a flashing light set in the top.

"Mummy, no one will see mine there," Harry says, so I reach for it and give it back to him.

"Where would you like it to be, then?" I ask, blinking fast, sniffing.

Harry places his sugar packet in the middle, at the front. He steps back.

"Perfect," he smiles.

I kiss his head. I have to get out of here.

"Come on, Nancy," I say, tugging at her hand. She's staring, mouth still open, at a zoo with a toy lion inside a home-made cage.

DOLORES, COSMO AND STANLEY

MY DAUGHTER, JANIS, and her partner, Ian, work very hard: she's always telling me. So I run around like a whirling dervish looking after her son, Cosmo, while she sits on her backside in a warm office all day, *working hard.*

Problem is, I'm running out of steam. I'm 68. I should be doing Sudoku in my conservatory, drinking sherry at eleven in the morning and enjoying free bus travel across Kent.

Instead, I'm in a car park at a soft play centre, in the rain, at ten o'clock on a Tuesday morning, fighting with Cosmo's car-seat.

From the outside, it looks like some kind of neglected warehouse, the sort of place where shoot-outs happen in a Bond movie. Except it's got ladybirds with smiley faces painted into and out of the grooves of its corrugated walls. They've used indoor paint by the looks of it, it's fading and peeling, and somehow the ladybirds have a sinister look, like they're plotting my demise. Cheerful in a way that says, *We'll get you, later.*

My back's getting rained on, and the big cold drops go straight through my cashmere cardigan, making me shiver. While I struggle, Cosmo tries to lick my nose. I lean across and fiddle with a buckle, dodging his waggling, persistent tongue which is coated with Laughing Cow cheese. As he hits his target, Cosmo begins to moo and cackle, in tribute to the eponymous cow, I suppose. I heave him out of the seat and set him on the dirty, graveled car park floor.

"Take my hand, Cosmo," I say.

He starts to lick my palm. He always licks when he's happy. Having Cosmo is a lot like having a puppy. He must get all this exuberance of his from his father's side: Lord knows, my Janis was a surly, lethargic misery of a child at Cosmo's age. And other ages.

The woman on reception here has a face like a monkfish with PMT. I'm dreading seeing her, but as I pull the door open, I see there is a mature gentleman on duty today. He looks nothing like a monkfish. More halibut to my mind, which is to say, quite tasty. I'm glad I took the trouble to do my hair and put this lipstick on now. One could very easily give up on all that; use the constant risk of being licked as an excuse not to make an effort with one's hair or face or nails. Like my Janis.

The man on the desk is smiling at me. "Would you like to come and play?" he says.

"Not me - my grandson," I say.

"Yes - I meant your grandson," he says.

"Well, obviously," I say.

We're the first here. I always come early, before anyone else has a chance to nip in and smear bogies on anything.

At the snack shack, I order a coffee. They drop a teaspoon of cheap granules into a brown stained mug, add water that was boiled fifteen minutes ago and charge me £1.80.

Cosmo spots the Coke. "No chance," I say, "Not after last time. You can have squash and Wotsits."

"Wotsits!" says Cosmo, delighted: my daughter doesn't let him have them at home.

"I don't know what that orange stuff on them is," she once said to me.

"It's cheese," I told her, but she wasn't having any of it.

Well, I don't get my Sudoku and sherry; Cosmo eats Wotsits. We all have to compromise.

We choose a table, and I foolishly get out my magazine, hoping for a quick read. Cosmo has different ideas. Maybe it's the squash, or the Wotsits, or just being two, but he's got more energy than the Duracell bunny.

He's licking the table leg now. "Stop licking table legs!" I say. Honestly, the things I have to say when I'm with Cosmo. "Stop sticking socks up your nose!" "Don't post that cucumber!" "There's nothing funny about sausages!"

I follow Cosmo to the ball pool. He hurls himself into the blue and white balls without a thought for all the bacteria lurking in there.

Lots of balls have been thrown out of the pool, and I start tossing them back in.

"Nana, you're didding it again," says Cosmo, annoyed by my constant need to tidy.

"It's a ball pool, Cosmo, it's supposed to have balls *in* it, not *around* it." He laughs and throws a few more out.

I can feel someone watching me, and turn to see Mr. Welcome Desk leaning over his counter.

"Tidying up?" He says.

"You're new here, aren't you?" I say, taking in the slightly yellowed finger tips on his right hand. "There's usually that girl on the desk - the one who looks a bit like a-"

"My daughter, yes," he says, "I'm helping her out today."

I think to myself, yes, I'd smoke too, if my daughter looked like a monkfish. My Janis may be miserable, but she's always been a looker. Gets that from my side.

"Funny," I say, "I'm helping my daughter out, too."

"The things we do for our kids, eh?" He's smiling, and I'm quite surprised, because I like the way his sandy-grey hair is a total mess, shaggy and wavy and sticking up and out all over the place.

"Tell me about it. I should be doing Sudoku in my conservatory right now," I say.

"Have you got a conservatory?"

"No. I don't know how to do Sudoku either, now that I think about it," I say, as a blue plastic ball bounces off my right temple and Cosmo erupts into the wild laughter of a maniac.

"Perhaps I could teach you," he says, smiling so that I can see the tell-tale thin black line of a cap between one of his front teeth and the gum. He doesn't seem conscious of it, keeps right on talking with his smile still pulling at his lips. "I'm a bit of an addict," he says. "In fact, I'm at it right now," he holds up the puzzle book he's been scribbling in at his desk. "I could teach you, if you like?"

"Maybe," I say. Am I being propositioned in a soft-play centre?

Cosmo, oblivious to the sexual chemistry fizzing through the air between me and the scruff on reception, has other ideas. He hits me with a barrage of balls, laughing his little socks off. I try to throw them back in as fast as he hurls them out, but it's a losing battle. I decide for everyone's sake to remove myself from the area.

"Come back, Nana!" shouts Cosmo.

"I need my coffee," I say, sighing at the thought of the insipid excuse for a drink that awaits me.

But who am I kidding? It doesn't work like this with two year-olds. I remember when my daughter was two, she was hard work. I was exhausted by her. And she's still exhausting me today: she just does it by proxy now, through Cosmo.

Cosmo is heading for what they call the 'main-frame'. It's a maze of primary colour-clad scaffolding, incorporating tunnel slides, rope net bridges and a great deal of discomfort for anyone taller or heavier than a Munchkin.

Ten minutes later I'm purple-faced and sweating, puffing, groaning, and cursing my knees.

"Can't catch me, Nana!" squeals Cosmo, and he's right. He's getting himself into corners smaller than my pockets, and my thighs simply aren't built for this kind of terrain.

"Hold on a moment, Cosmo," I huff, dragging myself backwards and upside down, squeezing between two giant blue rollers like a space hopper through a mangle. I manage to get my head and neck through, but as my chest hits the rollers, it becomes clear I have a problem. With a mighty groan, I pull my shoulders and chest through.

"Alright, Nana?" my Grandson says.

"I'm fine, son. It's not easy when you're well blessed, that's all you need to know," I say.

But I am not fine. I am stuck with my middle between the rollers, and my head and my chest hanging out one side, and my belly and my legs dangling pathetically from the other.

"I'll pull you," Cosmo says.

"You're sweet," I say, as he begins to heave uselessly at my hands. They're too slippery for him to get a grip. "That's because you licked them again," I say. "Now you see why you must never lick hands." "Yes." He looks serious.

I can't hold my weight for any longer, and flop lamely onto the blue plastic covered mat below me. It's quite comfy, if I stay on my side. But the soft play centre closes in about six hours' time, so I'll need to move at some point.

Cosmo runs off.

"Come back!" I hiss. There are other families here now, and I don't want them seeing me stuck between these rollers. Next think I know, my feet are being kicked.

"What's going on?" I can't see round the rollers to identify my attacker. "Is that you, Cosmo?"

A boy, smeared with snot and chocolate, appears above my hip.

"What's your name?" I try to sound authoritative (not easy when you're stuck on your side in a giant mangle).

"Storm," he says, and begins to climb through the rollers, over my body.

As he places a socked foot on my forehead, I say, "Did you just say your name was *Storm*?" but he's gone, vanished into the sticky vinyl labyrinth.

Where is Cosmo? I wriggle and writhe, but it's useless. I really am stuck, and thoroughly exhausted. I vow never to help my daughter again. She really should start paying for some proper childcare. I'm too old for this game. I should be playing Sudoku in a conservatory!

"Are you alright?'"

It's the voice of the man from the welcome desk.

"Your grandson came and got me. Said you were stuck," he says.

"Did he? Sweet," I say, trying not to swear.

"Said something about you being well blessed and not easy," he says, and this time I do swear.

"Don't worry, we'll soon have you out of here," he says. I can't see his face, but I can hear his grin loud enough alright. I picture the capped tooth as I feel his hands on the soles of my feet. He begins to push, gently. Cosmo appears at my head end and begins to yank at my arm.

"Come on Nana!" He looks like he might cry.

"It's alright, darling, I'll soon be out. You did a wonderful job getting help," I say, wishing I were dead.

With a final push, I shoot out from between the clamping rollers.

"Geronimo!" I yell for Cosmo's benefit, as I fly sideways past my open-mouthed grandson like some helmeted fool from a canon.

The man from the desk has his face wedged between the rollers now and he's smiling at me with that tooth of his. "Number five," he beams.

"What? Am I the fifth person to get stuck here? They ought to do something about it if that's the case." I can feel a letter to the council coming on.

"No - number five - the perfume you're wearing. Lovely. My favourite."

"Oh. Thanks."

"My name's Stanley."

"Stanley? How nice to meet someone who's not called Blaze or Noodle or Domestos." Stanley disappears, then pops up again, just in front of me.

"How did you get there?" I say, disorientated.

"Oh, I know my way around this maze. I've chased three grandchildren for many hours through this pit of despair," he says.

"Do you know a quick way down?" I ask, adjusting my twisted bra strap.

"Follow me," he smiles, and holds out a hand to help me across a chasm. "Come on, Cosmo, let's get your Nana back down to earth."

We scramble our way back through the lurid, sweaty rubber-stinking puzzle.

"Awful, these places, aren't they?" says Stanley. "I prefer a garden centre, myself. Plants, fish, and speciality shortbread: much nicer."

"You're right. I've never got stuck sideways in a garden centre." I reach forward and touch Stanley's arm. "Thanks for your help back there."

"I was wondering," he says, fiddling his fingers together awkwardly, the same way Cosmo does when he wants more Wotsits or he's wet himself. "Would you like to come to the garden centre with me tomorrow morning?" He looks dead nervous.

"I have Cosmo tomorrow," I say, playing hard to get.

"We can take him to see the fish," he says, pulling at his hair.

"He'll lick the tanks," I warn him.

Stanley holds out his hand and helps me off the mainframe. "We could go to the café, and I'll teach you how to do Sudoku."

Top marks for effort, I think.

"Maybe." I throw him a lifeline.

"The café at the garden centre is in a fake conservatory - it's lovely." He's starting to sound hopeful. I flash him my killer smile and seal the deal.

"Sounds divine," I say, as I take Cosmo's hand and try to walk in a straight line out of the soft play centre. "Goodbye," my hand flutters a wave that I hope looks casual, but my limbs are trembling like a newborn pony's. I'm not sure whether it's from exhaustion or the heady romance of it all. "Until tomorrow," I call over my shoulder as we walk out of the door.

"À tout à l'heure" he replies, waving back. I've no idea what he means, but it sounds fantastic.

My hands are shaking more than ever and it takes a few minutes of clumsy clunking to get Cosmo strapped into his car seat.

Finally, I flop into the driver's seat and check my reflection in the mirror. I wipe the Laughing Cow smear from my nose, and we head for home.

Hair

SHE SITS IN the supermarket café with her husband and two sons. I observe them from my own table, hidden by the large plastic yucca between us. On my plate, untouched baked beans congeal around dry chips and a greasy sausage.

One of her boys, who looks about ten years old, wraps himself around her and kisses her dreary brown cardiganed shoulder. The other, a teenager, sits opposite, kicking the underneath of the table. She manages to return the cuddles of the smaller boy while reprimanding the larger one for kicking.

I find myself wondering which of us two would have been the disciplinarian: me or Jim?

He was a softy, deep down. Too soft, probably. That was half the problem, afterwards.

Her black hair is very thin on the top of her head. I can see the skin through it, bright between the hairs. I imagine her in front of her mirror, where she must surely pull daily at those lonely strands, massage that pink scalp and pray for thick, glossy locks. Maybe not even glossy; just more.

I bet she didn't look like that when she got married. Her husband is good looking. Not my type... Jim was my type. But I can appreciate a good looking man when I see one, and her husband's decent enough: chunky, good jaw line, strong nose and full lips. The older son coughs and he puts an arm around him, ruffles his hair.

It's a small gesture but it's enough to bring the tears to my eyes: it doesn't take much, these days. Parents give up so much for their children. I assume that's when her hair went. Mine dropped out in my pregnancy, but for me it came back again.

If I asked her, what would you rather have, your hair or your sons, I know what the answer would be. We give it all up for our children. It's no longer about us, *we* are about *them*.

I run my fingers through my hair: thick, wavy, silky smooth and glowing amber; my crowning glory, so I'm told. I'd sacrifice it in a moment. A flash. Just to have Lila here. To have the baby that Jim and I made with love, and that I grew inside me.

I ate so carefully, so wholesomely! I barely gained any baby weight. Which I was glad of, after I lost her.

Still born. Born still, but still born. There was still the pain to go through, the contractions, the wait, the anticipation, the fear and then the moment when our beginning was all over, and suddenly it was our end. Jim drifted away from me without my realising it was happening; looking at me made him too sad. He took his hurt away by himself and disappeared from my life.

I look at that exhausted, balding, overweight woman, and I am filled with an envy that burns, like a white hot coal in my chest.

I wish I had hair like her.

Finders, Keepers

RUBY'S PLAYMATE, MILLIE, is halfway down the road, walking to her shiny blue car with her flawless mother. They will drive back to their four-bed detached, where their organic veg box waits for them on the front step.

I turn from the blown double-glazing that forms our embarrassing lounge window, and that's when I see it, lying in the chaos of discarded dressing-up clothes.

A tiara.

It's much nicer than Ruby's tiara. The plastic jewels are sparklier, there's more of them, too. The pattern of fake silver filigree is finer, more delicate and ornate. This is no Pound Shop tiara. This one's got something of the John Lewis about it. House of Fraser, maybe even.

"Millie left her tiara," Ruby says, magpie-eyed. She whips it up before I can get hold of it. "Can I run out and tell her, mummy?" She's scanning my face, eyes flicking over my features, testing me.

"We'll give it back to her next time we see her," I say, looking only at the tiara.

"But she might be sad."

"Oh, Millie's got so many things, she won't even miss it."

"But this is her favourite. She told me."

"She'll cope." I put the tiara into Ruby's drawer. "It's ours now, for a while."

"Like my Tellytubby doll?"

"That *is* yours, isn't it?"

"No, it was Charlotte's. She left it here ages ago."

I look at her, disappointed by her great memory.

"And my princess ball?"

"We found that in the park. Finders-keepers."

"But that girl was crying. She was looking for that ball."

"That's right. Losers-weepers. That's how the poem goes. Now, come on, it's time for tea. I've bought those lovely Jamie Oliver fishcakes you enjoyed so much last week."

"Have we got ketchup?"

"Of course. Let's wash hands and come up to the table. Wasn't that lovely, to have Millie to play? Such a nice girl."

"Have we got peas?"

"Fresh as the day when the pod went pop! Let me see if I can find them."

My fingers scratch and slip between turkey dinosaurs, fishy bites and cheap ice cream, finally finding the peas leaking at the back of our tiny freezer compartment. I pebbledash green across the floor before getting any into the pan, but I don't swear. I've never sworn in front of Ruby. I don't let her watch Horrid Henry either. And I think you can tell, when we're around other people. She's very well behaved.

"Hello, peas!" she says, picking them off the floor and cradling them in her palm. "You can be my friends! You can sit and watch me have my tea!"

She lines the peas up along the side of her Charlie and Lola placemat, wriggles onto her chair and begins to sing to her new green pals. Oh, to be Ruby, lost in her own little four-year-old world, where peas are your friends and life is safe.

"We need to wrap Summer's birthday present tonight, ready for the party tomorrow morning," I say.

She looks at me, quick as a flash, peas forgotten.

"You're not going to give her Ruby's tiara, are you?"

'Of course I'm not! What a thing to say! I got her some play dough."

"Playdough?"

She's looking at me suspiciously.

"That's alright, isn't it? I mean, you love playdough, don't you?"

"Yes."

She looks back at her peas, but she's not smiling anymore.

"Would you like to write your name in the card?" I lean over her, trying to coax that smile back, keep her in that happy four year old world. Keep her there as long as I can.

"I'll try." She smiles again, and goes back to her chat with the peas.

After dinner, she scribbles in the card to Summer. It looks cute but a bit sparse. I fake a few squiggles of my own, to balance the pattern of her squiggles out a bit. This time next year I'll be signing cards for her with my left hand. It's true what they say about having kids: the days go slow, but the years really do fly by.

Before she hops into bed, we wrap the playdough set in frosty blue Disney princess paper and stick the card on with Sellotape: I always stick the card to the present so that people know we gave one.

"I hope Summer likes our present," Ruby says, wriggling deeper under her Toy Story duvet. I kiss her pale forehead, stare at those grey eyes. Her father's eyes, not that he'll ever know about them.

"Of course she will," I say. "I would have been over the moon to get something like that when I was four."

"Did you have playdough when you were little?" she asks, her serious face focused intently on mine.

"I never had playdough when I was little.'

"What did you have?"

"Telly, mostly. My daddy bought me some playdough, once, but my mother took it and wrapped it up for me to take to another little girl's birthday party. So I never got to play with it."

I look back at those grey eyes, and they're wet.

"What's wrong, Rube?'

"That's so sad, mummy, it makes me cry. "

"Now then, no need to cry. I was alright."

"But your mummy was so mean to you."

"But now I get to play with all your toys, and you've got lots of playdough!"

She brightens. She can change her mood so quickly, with no hangover from the previous emotions. I wish I could let go like that. I still have a bad head left over from my mother, and I haven't seen her for fifteen years now. You realise it when you have kids of your own, when you love someone else like that; it makes you see your own mother in a new light. Mean-spirited; tight-fisted; hard-hearted... no wonder my father got out as quickly as he could. He kept coming back to me though; he loved me enough to bear seeing my mother once a year, on my birthday.

"Rest now," I say, planting one last kiss on that smooth blue-white forehead. "Get your beauty sleep, so you look your best for the party tomorrow." The tears are on my cheeks before I've left the darkened room.

The morning of the party is wet and grey. Summer's house is a big old Victorian place, three storeys with a fat red front door. Stained glass prevents me from seeing clearly through to the inside, but I know how it will be: a huge, oak floored hall, which will be littered with buggies and bags. The stairs will have beautiful thick, creamy carpet on them, I just know they will; the colour of sheep on a Cornish hillside.

And they do.

A parent I recognize, but don't know the name of opens the door. She doesn't seem to recall me at all. I force the smile to come, faking excitement over being here. Ruby pushes backwards, trying to melt her body into mine out on the step. I push her shoulders and we enter. The woman who opened the door has disappeared, left us standing in the hall.

"Ru-" I say, and I'm going to say "Rude," but we're caught out by the lady of the house, the hostess with the mostest, the queen of tarts herself: Sophie (who clearly had her highlights done before the party this morning). I hope it sounded as if I was about to say Ruby.

"Ruby!" She smiles manically at us. "Summer will be so happy to see you… she's here somewhere." Her eyes drift to me, and she looks like she's just remembered something very important. "I'll just-" she says, and disappears.

Ruby looks up at me, and her eyes say: *will you be alright, mum?*

"I'm fine. Off you go," I whisper to her, giving her a nudge in the back.

She skips off to join the hyperactive boys and girls screaming, squealing and screeching. The house has been expensively knocked through to improve circulation, and the kids are certainly circulating, at top speed. I take it all in, and can't fight the urge to roll my eyes.

I take a deep breath and I walk, slowly - carefully - through to the lounge, where Boden-clad mothers exchange gossip about each other's husbands and compare house prices. With no husband of my own and a rented house, I don't have much to contribute. I could tell them how Ruby's dad has had a restraining order placed on him, so that he can't come back and hurt me anymore, but I don't think that'd go down too well, somehow.

I see Millie's mother is there, but she's one of them and doesn't acknowledge me. Sophie is suddenly in my face, smiling and holding a white porcelain mug up at me. "Latté?" she says.

"Thanks," I say, glad of something to hold, but she's already gone.

I stand at the edge of the group, ogling the room. It's all Heals, Habitat and Amtico: very tasteful. I suddenly realise what a cheap shit present the playdough is, and remember that Summer's mother bought Ruby a High School Musical cheerleader suit for her birthday, complete with pompoms.

Ruby's off with her friends; they're all screaming at the boys rushing around, racing past impressively mounted frames with pictures of perfect parents smiling somewhere sunny. The boys are popping balloons, making the girls scream louder. I almost drop my latté as two of the little buggers race past me.

"We're all raising total stereotypes, aren't we?" Sophie appears again, still smiling.

"How do you mean?"

"You know, the pink and the blue of it all; girls who squeal, boys who trash things."

"I think it just happens. You can't fight nature."

"Maybe," she says in a way that makes me feel certain she disagrees, and she moves on with her tray of blinis.

We go to a lot of toddlers' birthday parties. They're all the same: kids running riot, with the stressed out homeowner torn between wiping bits of pizza off their walls and impressing the other parents with tapas nibbles from Waitrose. The host is invariably barely holding it together, giggling with teeth bared like a maniac, clearly teetering on the edge of shouting at everyone to *just effoff*. Parties always remind me how much hate there is in the world.

I'm looking round the house, and realise that if I was on the telly, I'd be describing it as sumptuous. But it's not the décor that's doing it for me. It's not even the solid silver charm bracelet I see on the hall telephone table, dropped and forgotten about.

It's Summer's toys that I can't tear my eyes away from.

They're mostly wooden, seriously expensive. Adorable. I find my eyes roving around the room, thirstily drinking in the view. Wooden bookends, one shaped like a cat, the other a mouse: *cute*. A pink wooden castle, with small princess dolls, the real Disney ones, Snow White and her crazy colleagues, Ariel, Aurora and Belle, those sisters from Frozen, and even a proper little Cinderella carriage. It's genuine Disney too, I can see the logo.

I see the fancy dress outfits, spilling from a basket in the corner. They're all the official ones, too. And there's a flamenco dress there: *stunning*. I bet Summer never even wears it.

But it's what's on the window sill that makes me stop breathing for a moment. There are about forty Sylvanian Family figures laid out on the glossy white painted ledge that follows the square contours of the bay. There are rabbits, hedgehogs, dogs and cats. There is the ice cream parlour, with its tiny pastel cones of colour. There is the Bath-time With Mother set, and the Birthday Party Set: *beautiful*!

There's a mother trying to talk to me, but I barely hear her as I approach the bay and all its treasure. I get down on my knees and take it all in. Talk about a feast for the eyes.

When I was a kid, everything was second hand. Everything was cheap and crap. Barbie's always had felt-tipped watches already drawn on them, or their arms completely missing. My Girls' World had make-up drawn on her face in biro when I unwrapped her at Christmas. Even my shoes already had someone else's brown toe prints in them.

I used to long for my birthday, when dad would come to visit. He always brought me something new. A doll or a bracelet. I used to hoard his things away, safe in a box far under my bed, away from my mother's hands.

What I could have done with a set of Sylvanian families like this! I know all their names: the Beagle Dog Family, the Barker Labrador Family, the Darwin Monkey Family; I smile at the humour behind it all and let my eyes feast on the detail. It's so *real*! Except, of course, it's bunnies in dungarees and so on.

Behind me I hear a half-hearted rendition of Happy Birthday. Summer is ripping the paper off her presents, thanking no one, appreciating nothing. The boys are grabbing hold of presents and ripping at them too. Their mums are shouting at them, calling them darling. I've noticed that a lot: when these women tell off their kids they say no, darling, don't hit your friend with that stick and watch out, darling, you just kicked mummy.

It's my chance, while they're all busy. I look along the row. The best thing by far is the bunny with the ice cream parlour.

I glance back over my shoulder, then, as I stand, I palm the bunny and pop it into my cardigan pocket.

I move over to where they're standing, to watch them cut the cake. The kids are bouncing off the walls. I look for Ruby. I'd almost forgotten she was here. She's watching me, frowning.

I think maybe she knows about the bunny. I smile at her. She's still frowning. She just keeps staring and staring at me.

I look instead at the birthday cake. It's a big sponge skirt, with a Barbie sticking out of it. Pink, pink, pink. The boys are saying they don't want to eat a pink skirt-cake, and the mothers are all desperately ignoring them, ooh-ing and ahh-ing louder than their sons' complaints, and telling Sophie she's the most talented cake maker in town and she really should set herself up in business doing parties.

I've always found Sophie a tedious bitch. And actually, I loathe Summer, too. They're just *so boring*, all these people. I can't stand them or their nasty children. I suddenly want to get out of here more than anything in the world.

But I have to sit through pass-the-chuffing-parcel, musical-chuffing-statues and pin-the-tail-on-the-chuffing-donkey.

At last, the food is eaten, the cake is cut and lumped into Peppa Pig serviettes, and dumped into party bags full of cheap crap that will be broken before we are home and thrown away if I remember it tomorrow.

Sophie is thanking us all for coming. She's almost squealing with delight at the visible finish-line of her ordeal. Her eyes flick around the place, taking in the greasy finger marks, the smears of snot and chocolate and the raisins that have been trodden into the creamy stair carpet and look like tiny poos that might have been done by the Barker Labrador Family. They will have to be picked out carefully by her Eastern European cleaner, who has probably been booked to turn up any minute now.

We're halfway to the door when a small boy that I hadn't even noticed suddenly points a rude little finger at me and shouts, "She's got Summer's bunny in her pocket!" The hallway is suddenly silent; even the kids go quiet.

Slowly, I put my hand into my cardigan pocket and pull out the bunny.

"What, this? I don't think this is Summer's," I say, hot cheeks surprising me, voice shaking a little. "I think this must be Ruby's. I must've brought it from home."

"I don't have any Slavian families," Ruby mispronounces, making one mother say *Ahh,* as in *isn't she cute*? But no one else is ahh-ing. They're all looking at me.

"Well, if it's not yours, how did it get into my pocket?" I ask, and I have no idea where I'm going with this.

"You took my bunny!" Summer suddenly shouts, and then she turns to Ruby. "Your mummy took my bunny!"

And then Millie pushes to the front of the little gang. "She's got my tiara at her house, too, and my mummy said she would never give it back and she hasn't, too!"

Ruby starts to cry.

"Here, if you're so sure it's yours, you have it," I hold it out to Summer. "But I'm pretty sure it must've come from our house."

"I did a circle on my bunny's foot." Summer turns the rabbit upside down, inside my chest my heart flips with it. "Here! Here it is! "It *is* my bunny. You took it!"

They're all still looking at me, and Ruby's sobbing now, quite loudly.

"Here, Ruby," I say, reaching out for her, but she won't come to me. "Come on, *darling*," I say, and I pull her by the shoulders towards me. "Thanks for having us, we had a *lovely* time," I say. "Sorry about the confusion over the rabbit there, I must've got it confused with one from home, or maybe another child put it in my pocket. That must be what happened."

They all stare at me blankly, mums and kids. I see the raised eyebrows, and I remember all the hate in the world. We turn and walk away. Ruby is sobbing and sobbing, her cries are making her bend double as she walks and I try to pull her upright by her arm.

"If you keep crying like that you'll make yourself sick," I say.

I can feel them still standing there, watching us in silence.

"If you're going to be sick, try and do it into your party bag," I say, loudly.

She stops and pulls her hand out of mine, crouches down, coughing and crying and smearing snot across her face with her sleeve.

"Come on," I say, still feeling their eyes on my back, "We're out of there now, everything's ok."

I reach into my pocket and rub my fingers back and forth across the little ice cream cones set I have there. It's perfect, the real thing in flawless miniature.

Play Date

I PRESS MY head against the box room window and watch the steam from my nostrils mist the pane. I've been waiting for ages.

At last I see them, as they pull up in their silver car, fiddle with seat belts and bags, climb out and finally make their way up our cracked front path.

"Kids!" I yell, "The girls are here!"

I have visions of my two dancing in delight, only I don't hear them moving from the lounge where they're watching the telly.

Well, I'm delighted, even if they're not. A play-date equals no effort on my part, and lots of activity for my two. It's a win-win.

I heard on the radio last night that research is starting to prove now that too much screen time zaps kids' brains and turns them into dozy little zombies. I'm not going to let that happen to my two.

I open the front door.

"Hello, Trish," I say, and then, in exaggerated tones that make me sound like an imbecile, I gush wildly at Kitty-Anna and Lilly-Rose, our little play-date-play-mates for the day. "Hello, girls!"

They greet me with appropriate stand-offishness. I'd be stand-offish too, if someone smiled at me like I just smiled at them. They hesitate on the doorstep.

"In you go then, girls," Trish pushes them from behind, tipping them over our doorstep and into the realms of my responsibility.

"What are you up to today?" I ask, holding her here against her will.

"Oh, I'm just off into town. Thought I'd get my nails done," she says.

"How lovely," I smile, thinking, *cow*. "Come on then, girls, in you come. Have a lovely time, Trish," I say, but she's already gone when I look up. I sigh and drop my voice three octaves. "Come on then, you two, out from there," I call into the lounge. I raise my eyebrows at Kitty-Anna and Lilly-Rose. "Honestly," I say, "What are they like?" Of course, our little guests have no idea how to reply to this. I go and turn the telly off and waft George and Evie out of the lounge. The four of them stand, small and uncertain, in the hallway. "Off you go and play," I say, then I turn and walk (although I'd rather run) to the kitchen.

It takes just thirty seconds for George to appear, dragging his socked-feet along.

"Mum, I've got nothing to do."

"Well you're not watching telly," I get in there quickly.

"But I'm so bored. Can I chop onions with you?"

"How can you be bored? You've got so many toys to play with. And this knife is too sharp for you, I'm afraid."

"Kitty-Anna doesn't like my toys; she just wants to do ballet. I did use that knife before, with Dad once."

"Oh. Well, maybe you could try and do ballet with Kitty-Anna? And I don't think you can have used *this* knife; it really is *very* sharp. What was Dad letting you cut that meant you were using this knife?"

"I don't want to do ballet. It was an apple."

"Well I expect Daddy was holding your hand and the knife together. She must like something else?"

"No, really, she doesn't; I asked. She doesn't like anything else at all. And I was just holding the knife myself."

Kitty-Anna comes pirouetting into the kitchen, stops, bows, coughs and scratches her head.

"You alright, Kitty-Anna?"

"Yeah, just a bit itchy. It's my nits. Mum says I've got millions. They just won't go this time." She coughs some more.

I put the knife down.

The girls are in the lounge, screeching along to the karaoke machine, fighting over the microphone. At least they're doing something, not just passively slobbed out in front of the screen.

I hear footsteps dashing upstairs and realise that George has ducked out of this one, and is keeping a low profile. I follow him up the stairs.

"You alright, George? Why aren't you playing with the girls?"

"I don't wannoo," he says, looking at the carpet.

"*Want* to," I correct him. He pulls at his jumper and rubs one toe against the opposite calf. "Is everything alright, George?"

"I just don't want to do karaoke."

He turns and walks into his bedroom, pushing the door shut between us. I stare at his door for a minute: at the picture of 1960s Batman and Robin over which George has scrawled NO GELS ALOWD.

I turn and head back downstairs, tiptoeing past the lounge and its awful barrage of screaming.

"Mum?"

They have this sort of radar, my kids. They can tell when I'm within ten yards.

"Can I have something to eat?"

"You know where the fruit bowl is," I say, and keep walking, hoping I'll get away with that answer. Nothing happens for the next five minutes, so it seems that I have.

Evie and Lilly-Rose have finally stopped screeching and gone upstairs. I'm pulling the washing out of the machine, trying to work out whether I've got enough radiator space to dry it on now that the rain's hammering down outside, when I have a thought: they've gone awfully quiet. Probably worth a quick check.

I find them camped out in my bedroom, cross legged on my cream carpet, my make-up bag emptied out onto the floor. Kitty-Anna is sitting with them like a perfect disciple, watching closely so that she remembers everything. Blue, brown and green powders have been gouged out and smeared across their faces. They have red lipstick cheeks and pink lipstick lips. They've drawn glasses and moustaches on with my new jet black liquid eyeliner. Earrings hang randomly in their hair and my necklaces are twisted around their arms. They're so absorbed they don't see me at all. Evie is holding her breath while trying to apply mascara to Lilly-Rose's eyebrows, and Kitty-Anna's leaning in almost as close as Evie. The carpet's covered in scraped patches of sparkle and coloured grease.

On the plus side, they are quiet.

I back out of the room silently. I'll save my voice until Lilly-Rose and Kitty-Anna are gone. Baby wipes should get the muck out of the carpet. Really, it could be worse.

I need to get downstairs without being heard, so I swing my leg over the banister and slide down, hopping off lightly at the bottom. In the kitchen I make a cup of tea and cry as quietly as I'm able to without attracting anyone's attention.

This is the problem when the telly goes off: your house gets trashed.

They're in the lounge now, watching a Peppa Pig DVD. I silently thank God for Peppa Pig and peek around the edge of the door, into the gloom: George is lying, face down, on the sofa. Kitty-Anna squats on the floor by his feet, skirt up, pulling at her knickers while staring at the screen.

I sneak away, hoping to remain unseen: no such luck.

"Mum-"

How does he do that? It's like a super power.

"Can I have a drink?" His words are almost slurred.

"Of course darling. Milk or water? What about you, Kitty-Anna? Would you like a drink?"

Kitty-Anna coughs deeply, and switches her stare from the screen to my face and back again, fingers still pulling at her underwear in a way that makes me want to force her to go and wash her hands and put a pair of trousers on before she touches any surface in my house.

"What?"

"Drink, Kitty-Anna. Would you like one? If so, what sort of one would you like?"

"Milk," she and George both say, and I groan, because milk's the worst stain for odour.

I'm waiting, with my face pressed to the glass of the box room window again. My nostrils make the same steam heart that they did just a few, long hours ago. I spot Trish fifty yards away, meandering up the road.

By the time the doorbell finally goes, I'm waiting on the inside to pull the handle and get those girls out.

Around me, the house looks like it's been burgled. There are Wotsits ground into the carpet, there's dried green fondant icing up the wall, and strawberry jam on the curtains over the patio doors.

The hallway is filled with every pair of shoes in the house, each with a cushion or pillow balanced on top of it. Someone's done an almighty, pipe-blocking turd in the downstairs loo, and someone else has missed the toilet entirely and peed all over the floor.

George coughs - it's the same cough Kitty-Anna's been barking the whole time she's been here. Evie scratches at her hair. I take a deep breath and pull the door open.

Trish is all smiles, looking fresh as a daisy. "Been alright?" she says.

"Oh yeah, they've had a lovely time,' I say, looking into the lounge, where the four of them sit, open-mouthed at the wonder of Scooby Doo. "Haven't you had a lovely time, kids? Come on then," I don't wait for the answer, "Come on, Kitty-Anna and Lilly-Rose, time for you to go now." I start scrabbling through the debris in the hallway, trying to find their shoes and coats.

"No rush," Trish says.

Sure, no rush at this end of the play date. "Oh, that's alright," I say, knowing my reply makes no sense. I only know I have to get those kids out of here as quickly as possible. "Come on, Kitty-Anna, come on Lilly-Rose, your mummy needs you now - she's missed you while you were here." *Yeah, like a boil on the backside.*

I go into the lounge and turn the telly off: groans rise up in unison, the only proof of life in the room. "I don't want to go," Kitty-Anna whines, breaking out into another lung-wrenching coughing fit.

"Me neither," Lilly-Rose joins the gripe, eyes still fixed to the blank screen.

"That's classic, isn't it?" I say to Trish, "They always get into something just as it's time to leave. Don't worry, girls, you can borrow the DVD. In fact, I'll give it to your mum right now and you can watch it at home and bring it back to us one day next week." In two strides I'm at the telly, popping the DVD draw open and causing more groans as George and Evie declare that this is their favourite and best DVD and they want to keep watching it when the girls are gone.

I grab four unfamiliar shoes from the hall and go back to the lounge. Trish leans against the door frame, phone in hand, checking her Facebook feed and tutting. Kneeling in front of Kitty-Anna, I grip her right foot and force it into the Dora Explorer shoe, sticking the Velcro strap down extra tight.

"That's the wrong one!" she complains. She's probably right, it was very tight. I ignore her and force the other shoe onto her other foot.

"You next," I say to Lilly-Rose.

"I'll do it," she rushes to put her own shoes on.

And still Trish lingers.

"That's it, girls, take Mummy's hands," I say, which they do, bless them, forcing Trish to put the phone back into her pocket. "Aren't they lovely?" I say to Trish. "They really have been good as gold." I pull the front door wide open and step outside in an effort to draw them from the house. They've forgotten the Scooby Doo DVD, and I don't remind them.

Inside, Evie and George have put the telly back on and are watching Charlie and Lola. They have forgotten poor old Scooby Doo.

I wave goodbye to their playdates, and turn to face the fallout.

WHAT A WAY TO GO

KATY'S GONE QUIET, and that's the time to worry. I should have registered it sooner, but I've been sniffing candles.

The truth is, I've been conducting a three year love affair with this garden centre. I have made myself at home in its bizarre combination of puppets, craft materials, conservatory furniture, mugs, scarves, cheap books, old-lady-shoes, pic-n-mix and scented candles. I feel so safe in its café, surrounded by the retired and the very young; those of us with time to kill. I love the gentle music and the enormous canvas pictures of cactus plants.

I thank God for Venus flytraps, and the hours Katy and I have spent playing tricks on them with a biro, poking their shiny red inner parts and making them close up for our entertainment.

I thank God, too, for their swinging sofa chairs, and the precious moments of oblivion I've spent on them, eyes closed, swinging back and forth with Katy happy.

I love the fish section, despite the horrendous heat in there; it's got me through many a rainy day in one piece.

I adore their Easter displays, and the way they hide fluffy bunnies around the place for desperate mothers like me to hunt out.

Best of all, I love their Christmas decorations: the tunnel of fairy lights they set up; the cheesy Christmas scenes with the fake sickly yellow candlelight glowing through the tiny plastic windows of tumble-down cottages and churches that Katy loves to touch and wonder at, and the momentary release for me as I am freed from demands to let my mind roam.

Our garden centre always has a grotto. We've never been in it (not yet, anyway: Katy's still terrified of Santa), but it has a musical band of automated bears that move their furry arms alternately up and down with a constant whirring drone, as their drumsticks fail to make contact with the plastic drums attached to their bodies. Katy loves that, and because she loves it, I love it. There are reindeer too, emitting the same, tired whir, as their heads go up and down, noses peppered with statically charged pods of polystyrene snow.

But I've got carried away, sniffing this cinnamon and cranberry wax concoction: something's happened down at Katy's height and the silence means it will be bad.

I look down. Her pale pink Hello Kitty leggings have a newly added dark pink centre, running down the inside of each short leg from crotch to ankle.

"Oh, Katy," I sigh. I don't have spare trousers in my bag. We're going to have to go home.

She begins to scream.

Katy never cries; she only screams. The problem with screaming is it prevents its audience from feeling sympathy, and instead makes them only wish the screamer would shut up. Crying equals pain and results in kindness: screaming equals bad temper and results in irritation.

I close my eyes for a moment, wishing I could block the screaming out, hush her up somehow, but I know there's no way: you can't shout someone quiet. She won't let me hug her. She just has to blow herself out. I bend my knees to get my head nearer to hers, and on the way down, I spot a small oval of brown next to Katy's shoe.

I frown: it's a familiar object, but out of context... and then I realise: it's a poo.

What am I supposed to do with that?

I consider toeing the poo under the display rack in front of us. The scent of the candles might cover its odour for a while - certainly until we're well out of the way. I look over my left shoulder, then my right.

There's an elderly lady within view. I can't do it. Instead, I rifle through my bag and find a supermarket till receipt. Gently - so gently - I hold the receipt over the poo and pick it up. This has the unforeseen but welcome effect of stopping Katy's screams. She watches me lift the poo, fingers touching the receipt as lightly as possible, and her eyes follow it all the way to my coat pocket, where I place it and let go with extreme care.

"Poo!" She says.

"Yes," I reply, "Poo."

"Not mine," she says.

That's a risk I'm going to have to take.

At home, with the poo carefully lifted from my pocket and dropped into the toilet, and Katy in clean, dry pants and leggings, I start on lunch. It's good to give toddlers choice, I was reading today, but choice over things that you don't mind about; the small stuff. Makes them feel like they're in control, when they're not. That's what I read.

I lift the wooden lid of the bread bin.

"White or brown?"
"Bown."
"Crusts on or off?"
"Off."
"Off?"
"No, non."
"On."
"No, no, no, off!" she shouts, as if I'm some sort of idiot. My own mother would say that I am an idiot, simply for giving the girl a choice. But she's not here to have a go at me, because, as she reminded me just yesterday over the phone, she's done her time and won't be an unpaid childminder. And anyway, like I said, the book I'm reading says it's good to give children simple choices, that it builds confidence. And what could be simpler than choosing how you have a sandwich?

"Butter?"

She's looking at me, but her eyes are glazed over, no doubt seeing some kind of bejeweled pink pony prancing through a land with marshmallow hills and chocolate flowers.

"Butter?"

Or can she hear me really, and she's choosing to ignore me? She pulls at her thin, yellow hair, scraped into even thinner bunches.

"BUTTER?" There's a growl in my shout. The neighbours will have heard that. They must think I have some kind of food-related Tourette's syndrome, I'm constantly shouting words like MILK? or HAM? at top volume in an aggressive tone.

"What?" She says, still out there with the ponies.

"Pardon."

"Pardon?"

"Butter?
"No."
"*Thank* you."
"What?"
"No, *thank* you."
"No *thank* you."
How can a three-year-old sound so sarcastic?
"Are you sure?"
"What?"
"Pardon. Are you sure you don't want butter?"
"Yes."
"Yes, *thank* you. Because it will be too late to change your mind after I've made your sandwich."
"Yes, butter."
"Right. Jam?"
"Bits?"
"Yes."
"Yes bits or yes no bits?"
"There's no bits of recognisable fruit in there."
"Good. No like bits."
"I know you don't like bits."
"No, no no bits. Bits give me rightnares."
"The bits in jam do not give you nightmares."
"Do."
"Whatever. Now, do you want me to cut your sandwich into squares or triangles?"
"Trangles."
"You sure?"
"Trangles."
"Ok, it's done. No going back now. Pink plate?"
"Of course pink plate." She rolls her eyes.
"Pink plate with spots or pink plate with Barbie?
"Spots."

"Here we are."

"I want fork."

"A fork? Why would you eat sandwiches with a fork?"

"I want one!" That's a scream threatening right there.

"Ok. The fork with the fairy on the handle? Or the one with the princess?"

"Pincess."

"Ok."

"No, no, no, fairy. Fairy, fairy, FAIRY!"

"Fairy."

"Yes."

"Right, sit yourself down then. Where are you going to sit? Sofa or table?"

"Sofa."

"It's such a nice day, you could sit in the garden."

"Sofa."

"You're sure?" But she's already on her way to the lounge. I follow, like a poodle. "Ok - here's your sandwich."

She looks at it for the briefest moment, and her face flushes almost purple, and her mouth contorts.

"AGHHHH!"

Tears are being squeezed from the tight corners of her small eyes.

I pick up the plate and slam it back down hard, *whump!* on the sofa, so that one of the sandwich triangles jumps off onto the rug.

"What's wrong with it?"

"I hate crusts! I hate butter! I hate jam! I hate brown bread! I hate that plate!"

I'm trembling. Without a word, I turn and walk out of the lounge, down the cool, dark hallway to our tiny under-stairs toilet. I go in, I sit on the toilet and I lock the door.

The inside handle of the door pretty much touches my nose.

I start to cry. Not much sound comes out. I open my mouth wide, my lips stretched tight, and I sob, making sounds like a hoarse sea lion at the circus, ball balanced on its nose.

She comes to get me, this daughter of mine who can never be pleased. She bangs on the door with those mean little fists of hers; those fists that take, take, take. She kicks at the door:kick! Kick! Kick!

"Mummy!" She shouts.

I breathe in. I haven't breathed in for what feels like minutes. I swallow my sobs. "What?"

"I need the toilet!"

"Why don't you go to the upstairs one?"

"I want *this* one!"

"Ok, ok."

I get up, scrape at my face with some hard toilet paper, and open the door. She doesn't realise I've been crying.

"Help me!" She sounds like the Lady of the Manor talking to the scullery maid.

I help her with her clothes, sit her on the toilet. I wait while she pees. She looks up at me and smiles. "I was just in time," she says, pleased with herself. "My pants are still dry. No accidents this time."

"Well done," I say. Now I'm the one being sarcastic. "That's great, good job."

"High five, Mummy," she says, palm up, ready for a clap to pass between us. I meet her palm without much energy.

"Come on then, come and eat your sandwich."

"I'm not hungry now, mummy. Can we go to the park?"

Thank God it rained, and I didn't have to endure the park for long. There's nothing more soul destroying than pushing a kid in a swing, them demanding, "Higher! Higher!" while you wish you could just shut your eyes for five minutes or sit down and enjoy a drink with no one touching you.

Back at home I take her rain-soaked clothes off.

"How about doing some dressing up?" I suggest.

We open the dressing up box and look at the tangle of polyester and gold thread; the pinks and the turquoises rubbing up against each other, cheap net skirts ripping and flowers dropping off.

"What are you going to choose?"

She doesn't speak, but pulls the dresses out roughly, not caring about the ripping noises.

"What about this one?"

"I hate that one."

"Shall I give it away then?" I put the blue Cinderella dress aside, remembering how she seemed to like it when we gave it to her for her birthday.

"No!"

"You don't like it, but you don't want me to give it away?"

"No!" She grabs it with strong, sticky fingers and shoves it back in the box.

"What about this one?"

"I hate that."

"Why are we keeping all these dresses if you hate them all so much?"

And that's when the screaming starts again. She begins to throw the dresses around and knock her ornaments over. This time, she's really pissed off.

And that's when the doorbell goes.

Jo doesn't knock very often, not these days. We both know why, although neither of us has talked about it with the other. Our lives seem to be running on different paths, hers full of work and success, mine full of Katy and tantrums.

"Hello," I say, the hesitancy already there in my voice. She looks as scared as I sound.

"I was just passing and wondered if you were around-"

"Yeah, we were just-"

"GO AWAY!"

"Hello, Katy," Jo says, sighing.

"Katy, don't talk like that."

Are there many friendships that survive the Terrible Twos? Will I survive the Terrible Twos? And why is it called the Terrible Twos when it continues into the threes?

Jo shrugs. "I'll drop by some other time," she says. She leans her weight onto her right foot and looks round the door at Katy. "Bye, Katy." Katy says nothing.

"Katy, what do you say?"

"Bye."

Sulky face. Folded arms. God help me.

The phone rings just as I click the front door shut. In the lounge I survey the mess: cushions on the floor, a banana skin dangling over the top of the telly, a glass, lying on its side in a pool of something wet and sticky on the sideboard.

'Hello madam,' the voice comes down the muffled line, sounding very far away, 'We are just conducting a survey…'

"GO AWAY!" I shout, before hanging the phone up.

I turn and see Katy, staring at me, eyes painfully wide.

"Naughty Mummy."

"Yes. Naughty Mummy."

I don't really care anymore.

In the kitchen, I put my favourite frying pan on the hob and light the gas. It sits there, warming, flat, fat and happy with the memories of a thousand spicy delights in its blackened surface.

I take two slices of white bread from the packet, and smear thick peanut butter onto one of them, and then spread a dollop of chocolate spread onto the other, pushing it across the porous surface like icing on a sponge cake. I stick them together, their brown-gold filling as thick as cement between bricks. I butter the outside of the bread, and lay it into the pan, which has heated through so that the butter sizzles on contact.

"What doing?"

"You still here?" I raise an eyebrow at Katy. She looks a bit dejected. She'll get over it. "Why don't you watch some telly?" She stands there, looking up at me. I lift her up to see the pan. "Mummy's making a sandwich, see?"

"Yuck."

"Yep. You wouldn't like it, that's for sure. And you know how I know that?"

"How?"

"Coz you don't like anything." I drop her down my body, back to the floor. "Now, off you go and watch telly."

She doesn't say anything, just stands there. I know she's confused by me right now, but I can't seem to change direction.

I turn the sandwich over. It's beautiful: crispy golden-brown, a little chocolate and peanut butter oozing out of the sides. I have a vague memory of learning somewhere that Elvis used to eat this very sandwich... where did I read that?

I think of Elvis, dying on the toilet, eating a burger. What a way to go.

When the second side is almost crispy and I can't wait any longer, I slip my ugly melted plastic spatula under the sandwich and flip it onto a plain white plate. I take the plate and, to my own surprise, put it on the floor by the dining table. I get down on my hands and knees and crawl under the table, then sit cross-legged and lean across my lap to reach for the plate.

Katy watches me for a moment, then crawls in after me. Her face is serious.

I bite into the sandwich: it's hot, and I open my mouth to draw in some cold air, making puffing sounds. Then I clamp my jaws down on it, burning my tongue and the roof of my mouth. I bite, and I swallow. The creamy, buttery goo feels good.

"You sound 'sgusting," Katy points out.

"So do you," I say.

I realise the only place I have any hope of being alone is the garden, with the back door to the house shut.

The telly is on indoors. I have plonked Katy onto the sofa hard enough to hopefully have wedged her in there between some cushions for a good while, and I am free. Chilly, but free.

I look around at the flowers and the weeds, growing together, and I can't tell good from bad. I begin to pull at them all, throwing them over my shoulder without looking back, making a pile on the grass. I'm not wearing gloves, and my hands are soon bearing the rope-burns of thick stems pulled too hard and too fast.

Katy appears at the back door. "GO AWAY!" I shout.

"Mummy-"

"Watch telly! Go on, watch it!"

She disappears back into the house. I can't see what I'm doing, it's all a blur, and now the tears are streaking down my cheeks, falling onto my shoes and into the earth. I pull and I pull, and something I've pulled up tickles my nose. I sneeze and realise I am desperate for the toilet.

If I go in there now, to the toilet, I will have to pass Katy, and if Katy sees me, the demands will follow. And then I'll be trapped, fetching, carrying, and having to hatch a new escape plan.

Well, I'm not going to do it. I'm not going in there. I make the rules here. This is *my* house. *I* draw the battle lines. I am the one who gets to choose.

I pull at the top button of my jeans and wrestle the zip down, my cold fingers stinging at the scratch of the metal teeth. I yank my jeans and knickers down to my knees, pulling them hard against my pale legs, and I squat, surrounded by steam as the hot pee streams out into the flowerbed.

WORKING FROM HOME

SIMON MISSED BEN'S nursery school sports day. He heard from his wife what a hilarious romp it had all been. He pictured her, heavy-bottomed and thick-ankled, thudding across the nursery garden, carrying their son on her shoulders; in his mind, Ben's fist was raised in triumph, as the other parents roared their support. He pictured each race she described, and saw in his imagination all the dads who'd been there: he lined them up for their amusing skipping race, with their woolly hats and mittens on, laughing and simultaneously feeling stupid and yet strangely attractive on display for all the mums to admire.

He felt the hole in his heart where sports day should have been. The hole began to hurt so much that, a week later, he considered booking a day off work - unheard of - so that he could be at his daughter's infants' school sports day.

Simon worried about missing a day's work: redundancies were being made in the firm, and he didn't want to look less committed to the office than those in the seats around him. His wife told him sternly that, in forty years' time, his boss wouldn't remember where he had been that Thursday in July, but that his daughter would always remember that her dad came to see her run.

Still, the worries tugged at Simon's neck. Thoughts of his boss and his mortgage smashed against each other until they made his head hurt and in the end he decided not to take the morning off, but to work from home instead. His wife agreed that she would phone him when Charlotte was going to be racing. They lived just one street away from the school, and he was a fit man himself. He would run straight there, thus managing to get his work done and doubling up to enjoy the fun of sports day with everybody else.

"It's the perfect work-life balance," he'd smirked, pen in hand as he watched his wife walk down the front path. He shut the door and turned back to the paperwork covering the dining table, the laptop rising out of the flood of charts and graphs like the Lady of the Lake.

His wife had barely been gone five minutes when she rang him.

"You'd better get here quick," she said. "Charlotte's just been called up."

Simon left an email half-written on his laptop, and ran from the house. Down their Victorian terrace, over the road and through the school gates he sprinted, his tie blowing over his shoulder, dashing around the side of the tall red brick school building, past the old entrance marked "BOYS" and round to the field at the back. He saw his wife immediately, standing away from the crowd.

"You missed it," she said, and her eyes looked wet, and her jaw looked very square.

"I didn't?" Simon puffed, hands on knees.

"You did."

Simon looked down at the dry, dying grass. A tear fell straight from his eye to the ground, like a massive single rain drop. He remembered as a child thinking that rain was God crying, and sunshine was God smiling. And thunder was God being grumpy.

He kept looking down. His wife touched his back briefly, then pulled her hand away.

"You should have come when I came," she said, sounding as if she'd known this would happen all along.

"Well then why didn't you tell me to come then?" He wiped his nose with the back of his hand.

"I did. You were on the computer. I knew you weren't listening to me." She put her sunglasses on and looked up at the unrelenting stretch of bright blue above them.

Simon sniffed.

"I'm a rubbish dad, aren't I?"

"Don't worry about it." She touched his arm, but her voice was tight and cold, like she was forcing herself to say the words against her will.

"How did she do?"

"Charlotte?"

"Yes. Where did she come?'"

"Hard to tell, too many heads in the way. She was one of the first three, I think. She ran well."

"She's a natural sprinter."

"So you've said before."

"Light and fast. She's got the right frame for running."

"She certainly looked light on her feet."

"She floats!"

Simon had taken Charlotte out running with him once, and had been stunned at her natural ability. It had freaked him out to see a six year old run so rhythmically, so effortlessly, like she was born to do it. Her reading, writing and numbers were tangled and slow and painful to eke out, but when she ran... when she ran, she did it right.

"Don't be too hard on yourself, Simon. She'll be in another race soon. Look, she's seen you, she's waving."

Simon waved at Charlotte. She was wearing a silly pink hair band with a huge bow on it. She looked like some kind of milk-white Minnie Mouse, all arms and legs, grinning a huge, gappy smile at him. He waved madly, almost unselfconscious, shouting her name and feeling like a real dad for a moment.

"When's she running again?" he asked his wife while he carried on with the crazy thumbs-ups and waves. He was enjoying getting into this role, Dad with a tie on, the dad who takes time off work just to see his kid run, that great dad, you know the one... He imagined the teachers in the staff room later, saying wasn't it nice that Charlotte's dad came, he obviously had a lot of work to do, so wasn't it doubly great that he took that time out for his daughter?

"Don't know." His wife was rubbing sunscreen onto her already pink nose. "There are loads of races. It's really bad luck you missed hers."

He realised with a desperate and mysterious pain, somewhere between the physical and emotional, how desperately he suddenly did want to be that dad.

"Don't worry," his wife said. "It won't be long. She'll run again in a minute, I'm sure."

So he stood, with the other parents, bored behind the line of rope, waiting, watching hundreds of kids he didn't know and didn't care about balance eggs on spoons, jump in sacks, bounce on space hoppers, dress teachers and fill water tubes. He could have got *so much* work done while he was stuck there, just waiting!

Finally, it was Charlotte's turn to run again. She was part of the relay. An older child led her to a point on the course and showed her where to stand, guiding her with their hands on her shoulders.

"Charlotte!" Simon shouted, hands cupped around his wide open mouth. She didn't hear him. "Charlotte!" He shouted again, and again, but she either couldn't hear him or she was ignoring him. She was making him look foolish in front of the other parents. Why didn't his kid respect him? "Charlotte!'

"Hang on! Is she crying?" his wife said, taking off her sunglasses.

Simon squinted at his daughter. She was rubbing at her eyes, and the older child was bending down, looking concerned. Charlotte's face and neck were the familiar blotchy red of an emotional meltdown of some sort.

"What's going on?"

"I guess she doesn't want to do it. I hope they'll make her do it." His wife scrutinised the small group of people gathering around her daughter, trying to calm her. Charlotte's sobs were now audible. People around them were starting to notice the kid with all the problems.

"For God's sake!" Simon hissed at his wife, "What's wrong with the girl?"

"I don't know any more than you do, Simon. She's six. I suppose she's just having a moment."

"That's your girl, isn't it?"

The fat man with the skin-head, piercings and tattoos, who was blocking their view as effectively as a brick wall, turned and accused them.

"Mmm" Simon looked away from him.

"That's my boy over there." The man pointed at a thin, shaven-headed boy with tattoo stickers all over his arms and both ears pierced. He looked about four. He was smiling, doing as he was told, clearly getting along with the other children very well. Smug little turd. Simon rolled his eyes.

"She don't look very 'appy, your girl," the brick wall continued. Simon ignored him.

"No," his wife said, "She doesn't, does she?"

"What's going on?" Simon gripped his wife's arm.

"That hurts!" She pulled away.

"I haven't stood here for an hour to watch my daughter make a public fool of me," he hissed.

His wife's voice was measured, careful and low.

"Then why don't you go back to work?"

"Good idea."

"You serious?" But even as his wife turned towards him, she saw he was rearranging his tie and straightening his trousers.

"Charlotte saw me here earlier, she knows I came. Let me know how this works out." He pecked his wife lightly, so lightly that he barely brushed her cheek, and walked away, behind the lines of parents and around the corner of the school, out of sight.

His wife watched him go and a coldness crept over her despite the heat of the morning. She tightened her lips and squinted at the place where he had been. She turned back to the race and was disappointed to see that the older child was walking Charlotte back to where the rest of the red team sat waiting. They had replaced her with a different red team member, one who was more emotionally stable under pressure. She knew that Charlotte would be disappointed with herself. They would have to talk about it after school, or at least, she would try and Charlotte would probably refuse to talk at all.

She knew that Charlotte would not race now. There was really no point in hanging around here. She turned and followed the route her husband had taken, leaving the school and Charlotte behind her.

She took her time going home; she wanted to make sure Simon had left the house and returned to the office.

Starting Small

I HAVE BEEN lying to my son for years and years and years.

Now, come on; don't look at me like that. You do it, too, don't you? Don't we all? Little things at first. It started small.

Like the day Ewan walked in on me in the bathroom, just as I was inserting a tampon.

"What are you doing, mummy?"

"I'm just changing my batteries, darling," I smiled.

Or there were the money-saving lies, like when the ice cream van went past: "The music means he's run out, love." Small lies, that grew.

Like the day the local paper came out, and the results were announced for the beautiful baby competition:

1st Place: Alfie Skipper
2nd Place: Skye Skipper
3rd Place: Jordan Piper

I scanned their pasty faces, bland smiles and empty eyes. What a fix. The town was full of Skippers, and they'd evidently been voting in force. And the Pipers were related to them, somewhere along the way, by marriage.

I take the large scissors from the kitchen drawer and cut around the picture of my boy, Ewan. He's on the third page of the four page feature, with the headline 'No prizes - but still adorable.' I hold his picture to the fridge door, and pop a magnet on it to secure it there.

Ewan skips in.

'What's that, mum?' he says, twisting the head of the Lego figure in his hands round and around and around.

"It's your picture. From the newspaper."

"Did I win?" He's already smiling. His world's still all cherries. I'm not going to be the one to turn it all to stones.

"You did," I say. It comes out so easily. Well, how can you tell a three year old they're not the most beautiful kid out there?

When I realised Ewan really did soak up every word I said as if it were gospel, well, then I began to really enjoy myself.

"Mummy used to dance with the Russian ballet." Ewan repeated my stories to his school friend when he came round to play.

"And you won't find me on YouTube, because it was long before all that existed," I say, laying a plate of Jammy Dodgers in front of them.

So it was Ewan who started spreading the lies. And then I started, too: little lies to everyone else. Like at the soft play centre, when I told a woman I had four children, not just the one.

She seemed a nice woman, too. But she had three children, and I feel it, you know: the smug stench from those women who've shelled more than two peas into the world.

Well, I was getting on with the woman, and I didn't want her scorn. So I embellished a little.

By then, Ewan had stopped contradicting me. He just went along with whatever I said was so. We took life second by second, living as the moment necessitated.

You're looking at me again, aren't you? I can feel it, you know, the rise of your eyebrows. But you can't judge me, because I know you lie, too. We're all at it. Of course, he lied to me about his exam results. Well, he tried to, but you can't trick a tricker. I saw straight through my boy. Found the letter, hidden under his pillow.

I wasn't cross. I mean, I did very well at school, but that's just me. I'm academic. People get intimidated when they hear I got a First from Cambridge. That's why I tell them I never went to university. To put them at their ease.

Or, hang on; maybe I didn't go to university, and I tell people I got a First from Cambridge... I can picture me being there, but to be honest, I can picture myself pretty much anywhere now. Nightclub singing on a cruise-ship; hostage negotiator in a tough, downtown L.A. neighbourhood; chief store detective at Harrods... There have been so many small lies over the years that I'm not entirely sure these days which ones were true to start with.

Ewan once asked me how it was possible that his Dad was still away on a world tour with a band he'd never heard of and could find no evidence for on the internet.

I hate the internet.

Lie upon lie, the years have passed. Now all I've got left to lie about is my age.

Now... now I know less and less about my boy.

He's nineteen now. Moved out. Won't tell me what's going on. He shares a flat with a boy called Kevin.

I still get post for him, though. Strange post. Final demands and threats through the mail.

And then there's the calls. Calls at all hours of the night. There's often a knock on my door somewhere between midnight and five. Shifty people who won't look you in the eye. Someone tried to break my door down, once. I told them, shouted through the letterbox at them, "Whoever you want, he's not here."

I saw him last week. Bumped into him in the supermarket.

"How are you?" I was desperate to know. My voice was shaking, and my hands, too.

"Alright," was all he could manage.

"I miss you." I gripped his arm.

"I'm alright," he mumbled.

Kevin was lurking in the background. He laid his hand on Ewan's shoulder.

"Come on," he said.

It reminded me of one time when Ewan was little, and we passed a car crash. "Come on," I'd said, my hand on Ewan's shoulder, just like Kevin's was now. I hadn't wanted my boy to be upset by the twisted mess of human life before him.

"What's with this Kevin?" I said to Ewan, perhaps a bit too aggressively. "What's his hold on you?"

"Nothing." Ewan talks to my shoes. "There's nothing going on, mum."

At this, Kevin hmphs and walks away, muttering something. A real pair of mumblers and shufflers, these two are.

Ewan looks at him, and me, and him.

"I have to go, Mum," he says.

But I'm no fool. I can see what's going on here. Kevin's clearly having difficulties and my Ewan's supporting him through them. Always was a good boy, my Ewan.

Well, that's just the way I raised him.

The Easy Option

LUCY PHONED DAVID, catching him just before he left the office.

"I've brought the kids to the supermarket for tea," she said, self-conscious amidst the listening ears of other customers staring into space and not talking to each other while they ate at the tables around her.

"Have we not got any food in?"

"Yes, David, we have got food in, but I cannot face the nagging, whinging, begging or crying. And, at the end of whatever pathetic excuse for a meal the kids actually eat, I want to be able to just get up and walk away."

If only David knew just how much Lucy wanted to walk away, far away, like, *air*-miles away from all of this.

"But I don't expect you to understand," she carried on, her tone brittle. "After all, you just come home and eat the food that appears like magic in front of you."

"Now, hang on Luce," David countered.

"No, no, I know what you're thinking. I can hear it, David, loud and clear: silly old Lucy fails again; failed cook, failed mother, failed wife. I hear you."

"But I never said…"

"And you might as well know that Megan's teacher says Megan isn't where she should be in the grand academic line up of five year olds, and the nursery staff are complaining that Jake is saying *poo poo* and *willy willy bum bum* to other children. Repeatedly."

David laughed in reply.

"That's not helpful." Lucy kept talking, although she barely recognised the scathing voice as her own. "And my Mum rang today and kindly pointed out my many and regular failings."

"Well I hope you didn't listen to her." David sighed, firmly in familiar territory.

"Oh, it's too late for that. I heard her and now she's there, David, she's in my head. *You never say no to them* was today's special flavour."

David sighed again.

Lucy closed her eyes and for one blissful moment, everything disappeared, and all she could see was a red-orange-brown mix of colour. Her retreat was broken by a sticky finger tapping the end of her nose.

"Gotta go. Maybe see you here?" She pressed the red button on her mobile phone, set it back down on the table and switched her attention to her daughter. "That's supposed to be your pudding, Megan." Lucy looked sternly at her daughter who was tucking into the pink iced ring doughnut. Megan ignored her. "I suppose that's my fault for letting you choose it before your main course arrived," Lucy sighed.

"That's right mummy. You shouldn't have let me have it," Megan said; five year old know-it-all. Lucy scowled at her.

"Thing is, Meg, that's how canteens work. You just get all your food in one go, and normal people wait to eat their savoury before they start their sweet. That's the thing, Megan, that's the thing."

Lucy folded her arms on the mottled melamine table top, stretching her elbows away from the edge where ancient ketchup and brown sauce globules solidified like sticky birthmarks. The soundtrack played Christmas songs, although Christmas was still two months away. She stared up at a huge canvas depicting fish and chips, with a lemon wedge balancing on greasy batter. A baked bean had somehow got stuck on to the picture, right in the middle of the lemon, and had dried there like a single piece of pebbledash.

"Mum," Megan began.

"No, Megan, I don't want to hear it." At last, Lucy felt the release of simply saying "No".

"But, Mum,"

"I said no."

Jake reached out from his highchair, caught hold of the triangular handle of Lucy's coffee cup and pulled it off the table. The cup hit the floor and exploded, sending lukewarm coffee and broken china in every direction.

"Jake!" Lucy jumped up.

"Mummy, Jake dropped your cup," Megan helpfully explained.

"Yes, Megan" Lucy looked for a member of staff. All around, frowning customers confirmed that Lucy had done a Very Bad Thing.

"I was trying to tell you he was reaching for your cup, but you wouldn't listen to me."

Lucy ignored her daughter, and kept scanning the canteen for someone who might help. They all seemed to have vanished, so she walked down to the food counter to grab some serviettes. Looking back, she saw Jake climbing out of the highchair with one leg almost reaching the table, but not quite. If he shifted his weight, he was going to fall straight down, cracking his head on the table edge on the way.

She sprinted back and grabbed him hard under the arms. "Ow!" Jake complained.

"Mummy, Jakey was climbing onto the table." Megan continued the running commentary of their lives.

"Yes, thank you, Megan."

Glancing down, she saw that Megan's hands and face were entirely covered in baby pink icing and sprinkles. Her nostrils were stuffed with icing; how could she breathe?

"You've got a bit of icing on your nose, Megan."

"No I haven't."

I wish I had her self-belief, Lucy thought, not for the first time.

"What's happened here then?" a weary voice sighed over her shoulder.

Lucy turned to see a middle aged woman squeezed into a green uniform, egg and ketchup stains across the striped tabard that covered her bulging front. She held a mop handle, which rested in an old tin bucket on a trolley. She dragged the grey ropey mop across the coffee and china mix, making scratching sounds on the tiled floor.

"Jakey dropped Mummy's drink and he climbed on the table." Megan brought the waitress up to speed.

"I needed serviettes," Lucy said.

"You can't take your eyes off 'em for a moment at this age," the cleaner said.

"If you had straps in your highchairs it would have been fine," Lucy said, picking up Megan's doughnut and taking a big bite.

"They're not *my* highchairs. I just work here," the cleaner said, her voice now flat and sulky.

"Number sixteen?" A spotty boy with piercings in his eyebrows, nose, ears, lips and tongue arrived with their food. Megan and Jake stared silently. His face turning poppy-red merely made him more interesting.

"Mum..." Megan began, but was silenced by Lucy's expression.

"Thank you," said Lucy, trying to lift the food over the cleaner who was now on all fours under the table, pushing the mess around with a grey rag.

"Here you go, Megan, sausage and mash."

"I don't like mash."

"Sausage and mash, like you asked for. Jake, here's your nuggets."

"Bollocks," Jake said.

The entire café seemed to fall suddenly silent.

"I'm sorry," Lucy wiped the hair from her eyes, "He's not saying what you think he just said. That is just how he says 'nuggets'. I know what it sounds like, but it isn't."

The spotty boy snorted, sniffing back what sounded like a few spoonfuls of snot.

Megan pushed her sausages around.

"Not hungry."

"You shouldn't have eaten the doughnut first," Lucy sighed.

"They eat what they're given." The cleaner's voice came from under the table.

Lucy ignored her.

"Mum," Megan said.

"Shhhh, Megan." Lucy aimed for distraction. "Eat your sausages."

"The lady under the table is talking to you."

"Yes, Megan, just eat your sausages."

"She's looking at you."

"For goodness' sake, Megan, just eat your bloody sausages!"

"No wonder your kids have got potty mouths, their own mum talking like that," the fearless cleaner continued.

"Mum"

"Megan-"

"She looks like Uncle Richard."

Thank you, God.

I looked between my knees at the cleaner.

"Yes, Megan, you're right. She does look like Uncle Richard. But it's not polite to say that women look like hairy fat men, OK?"

That shut them both up.

In the silence, Lucy bit hard on her bottom lip.

"I'm sorry," she began. "That wasn't very nice of me. I'm just - I didn't mean-"

Jake began choking on a nugget. His coughing was a frightening sound, wheezy and gasping.

"Bollocks!" Lucy shouted, panicking.

The cleaner tutted.

Lucy whacked Jake on the back. Hard. Very hard. She wasn't taking any chances. The nugget came up. So did everything else Jake had been nibbling on for the past few hours. Milkshake, peas, quavers, chocolate buttons, breadsticks, grapes, raisins, cheese. The whole lot shot out in a huge, lumpy shower of puke. It covered all of Megan's dinner and filled Lucy's handbag, which lay open on the table.

"OMG!" Lucy heard the spotty waiter cry from the other end of the café.

"Mum!" came a voice behind her. Lucy looked around instinctively. But she didn't recognise the tall, blue-haired teenager standing there, luminous yellow painted fingernails resting lightly on a bony hip.

"Jess!" The cleaner's voice had gone up an octave. "What are you doing here? You're supposed to be in an exam right now."

"I never went, alright?"

"You - what?" The cleaner heaved herself up from the floor and stood there, the broken handle of Lucy's cup in her fingers.

"I just didn't go. Can I have a tenner?"

"Why didn't you go?" The cleaner was fumbling through her pockets. "My money's in my bag in my locker."

"I wasn't gonna pass, so what's the point?"

Lucy looked at the teenager, and thought about how young people never realise how beautiful they are. And then she looked over at the cleaner. Their eyes met.

"I guess it doesn't get any easier," said Lucy.

The cleaner said nothing. She stared at Lucy. She stared at Jess. Slowly, she turned to Megan and Jake.

"Mum? I need ten quid," said Jess, kicking at her mother's bucket on wheels, nudging it back and forth with her toes.

The cleaner reached out and caught the trolley handle to stop the rocking bucket. Then she touched Jake's head and crouched down, so that her face was level with Jake and Megan's wide eyes. She stared at them. They stared right back at her.

"You two be good for your Mummy," she said, eventually.

"Yes, yes, we will!" Megan said, sounding like one of the children from Mary Poppins.

"Coz it's hard work being a mummy," she continued, her eyes meeting Lucy's just for a moment.

"Mum," said Jess, rattling the mop handle.

The cleaner stood up, and turned to walk away.

"Wait!" Lucy half stood, the backs of her legs trying to push out a chair that was bolted to the floor. The cleaner half turned to face her, and Lucy reached out to touch her arm.

"What?"

Lucy opened her mouth, desperately seeking the words.

"Mum," Jess insisted.

"Nothing," Lucy said, and let go.

"I'll get you some serviettes," the cleaner said, "To clear the sick up."

"Thank you," said Lucy.

"Well, you can't leave these two unattended, can you? Not without straps in the highchair." And she smiled at Lucy, a small smile of recognition. Then she went to get the serviettes, dragging her mop and bucket alongside her, while her daughter slumped along at a distance so that, should any other teenagers be in the supermarket, they wouldn't think her related to the cleaner.

Lucy turned to survey the carnage of their tea. Puke dripped from the table onto the floor.

"Oh dear," a warm voice spoke gently, and she could hear the smile there, and it made her smile too, even as the tears pricked her eyes. She turned to see her husband, his tie loosened, and his hair a bit of a mess.

"David, I'm so glad to see you! I'm sorry about earlier - how was your day?"

"Ok." David dipped his knees and tilted his head to take in the full scale of the disaster scene. "Yours?"

"Just dreamy," said Lucy, and began to laugh at the same time as a tear escaped and ran down her cheek.

"Daddy!" Megan jumped up in her seat. "I've been so lucky, you won't believe it!"

"Really? What happened to you?"

"Jakey puked up everywhere, and guess what?"

"What?

"It didn't get on me at all!"

Fish on Holiday

I CHECK MY watch: twenty minutes until Josh needs collecting from football, forty minutes till Elsie needs picking up from her playdate.

I'm never going to get everything done. I've got this list in my pocket to work through and I don't know what I was thinking even writing it, because I haven't got a hope of getting any of it ticked off. Tom pulls at my trouser leg.

I must find a present for my mother-in-law. And a card. That's the very minimum I must do from this list. If I can get them bought, wrapped and posted this evening, I'll be halfway there. So why am I standing here staring at these stupid fish?

Tom's pulling again, sticky biscuit fingers on my clean jeans. It is so hot in here. I stare down the corridor of glass tanks, each lit by a pale, thin strip above. The gormless fish drift aimlessly in their little cells.

"Ahhh luvooo, MumMum," Tom declares to my knee, little fingers gripping my calf hard.

What am I going to get my mother-in-law for her birthday? She likes cacti, but I can't post a cactus. She likes glass ornaments, too, but I can't post those either.

"One, two, free, five, free, one I cut a fiss alee," Tom sings to my thigh.

I hear my phone ping to signify the arrival of a text. Sighing, I rummage through my overstuffed bag. It's John.

Any luck with mum's pressie?

I ignore it, drop the phone back into the murky depths of my bag.

"Loveeee fisss," Tom's still singing, making it up as he goes along. His short arms reach up and I heave him onto my hip.

We point. We gaze. *Oooh. Ahhh.* Yeah, yeah, blah blah.

She likes books, my mother in law, but I don't know what she's already read. Maybe a cookbook? But some women feel insulted when you give them a cookbook. Don't go there.

Tom is stroking my cheeks, still singing. "Bootiful MumMum, lahley fiss, booful MumMum, lovee lovee MumMum…"

We're running out of time!

My phone pings again. I switch Tom onto the other hip and dredge my bag for it. My hand pushes through screwed up tissues, sucked and re-wrapped lollipops, toy cars, action figures, my open purse, escaped coins, pens, receipts, a small colouring book, my address book, a sock and a plastic tiara before it finds the phone. How did it fall so far, so fast? I check my text: it's John again.

Any luck?

I wish I'd never looked. I drop the phone back into my bag.

"Two minutes and we really must go," I warn Tom.

"No," he begs, lunging towards a fish tank to press his palms to the glass. Good job I had a tight hold on him.

"Wassiss?" He's running his hand over the tank's glass front. The fish inside are large, pale orange discs, but I see that Tom's looking, not at the fish, but at some handwriting scrawled in capitals on the tank: FISH ON HOLIDAY.

"It says 'fish on holiday'," I run my finger over each letter as I read it. And then I think about it, and I frown. "Fish on holiday?" Tom's looking at me intently, studying the way my mouth is moving. *"Fish? On holiday?* What on earth is that about?" I'm getting worked up now. More than is necessary. I don't know why. "What a waste! Fancy sending a fish on holiday! They're hardly going to appreciate it, are they? I mean, when did you last see a fish stop and smell the roses?"

I'm asking Tom, like a two-year-old has any idea. He nods, smoothing my hair with his sticky little palms.

"And seven seconds after their holiday's over, they'll have forgotten all about it! Honestly, how stupid can you get?"

"Stoopid stoopid," Tom sings. He plants a wet kiss on my forehead, I wipe it away with my sleeve.

I hoist my bag higher on my shoulder and put Tom down, take his hand in mine and start walking towards the cold air of the exit.

Mother-in-law. Mother-in-law. Mother-in-law. I must focus on my mother-in-law. The post office'll be closed now anyway, I realise, so a parcel will never make it in time. It'll have to be a voucher again this year.

"Come on," I say to Tom, who's stopped in front of some small bright fish. "Time's up!"

Something To Do

"IT'S THE END of an era," my mother declares down the phone. "A decade at home. You won't know what to do with yourself."

Standing in the surge of bodies at the classroom door, bobbing and swaying like seaweed in the tide of other parents jostling to witness their children taking those first steps into school, the worry of just what I am going to do with myself hits me. My hands hang loose, unused.

I want to stay at school with Tilda. She's so little. The other two were much bigger in their reception years. She's a June birthday, and it shows.

But she's so much fun: full of spirit and imagination. At last, by my third child, I finally learned to enjoy it all, and I don't feel ready to let go just yet. Tilda was my daily ticket to guaranteed giggling.

I amble home, dragging my feet like a teenager who's already late for school and who is eking out the journey in order to miss everything until break-time. I shove my hands in my pockets, for something to do, my left hand finding a broken button with a sharp edge to fiddle with, my right hand squeezed tight around my door key.

When I open the front door, the silence of an empty house rushes up to greet me. I push past it to the radio in the kitchen, click someone happy on, and grab the dishcloth. I scrape Weetabix and stuck-fast grains of sugar off the table.

What is Tilda doing now? Will her teacher have realised how bright she is, how able, how funny? Lots of people miss it, but it's there; something in the tilt of her chin, a certain look in her eye.

I think, I must load the dishwasher, but when I open it, I discover that I already did that. I fill the kettle and flick the switch; stand there waiting for it to start doing what it's made for.

The clock above the sink ticks louder than I've ever heard it before.

I take my coffee to the lounge, and slurp it noisily on the sofa. When I turn the TV on, it's on CBeebies, and I don't change it. I try not to find the presenter attractive and I fail. What's wrong with me, fancying a grown man dressed as an astronaut? I think about phoning Mum and decide against it.

At half past ten, after watching twin doctors explain how the sphincter works, I leave the house and drive slowly to the beach. It usually takes fifteen minutes from ours, but I make the journey last thirty.

The sea is a grey broth, a sludgy cauldron of boiling brine, aggressively throwing itself against the concrete flood defences. It has eaten all the beach. I don't care. I trot along the pavement, tapping my hand lightly on the rails as I go, feeling my fingers bend back with the pressure of each metal rod.

I see a dead seagull and I stop to examine it, bending over, careful not to let my scarf touch it. It's a young one, white feathers with browny stripes still not gone. Its eye is closed. I realise how bird-like my husband's eyes are when he's asleep.

"The seagull looks like Daddy," I say, laughing out loud.

A teenage boy shuffles past, staring straight at me quite unashamedly. I realise I am alone. I can't believe I've just called Tom *Daddy*, and giggle.

I hop-scotch the paving stones: well, they are pink and yellow, I can't resist. I pop into Tilda's favourite toyshop, a beautiful old fashioned, bow-windowed shop with red and yellow painted woodwork. There are racks and racks of jokes and toys. I buy a submarine that promises to both dive and surface when wound up in the bath. I can't believe it will actually dive. I mean, surfacing - that's easy when you're tiny and plastic. But diving's another matter: that takes weight; power; *drive*.

And then I see just the café for me. Right on the corner by the seafront. Adorable windows wrapping around the curve of the road, making the most of the views. I've often wondered about going in here when I've brought Tilda down to the beach, but always decided it looked a bit genteel to relax with a preschooler who has a habit of making observations at top volume.

I go into the café and examine the cakes behind the curved glass counter. There is a huge, round, white-iced Belgian bun. When I was at secondary school we used to walk to the bakery on the high street during our Friday lunch break, and I bought a Belgian bun every week for almost five years, only I used to ask for a Belgian *bum*, and think myself hilarious. At the sight of the plump, sweet iced bread roll, some long-dead sense within me is revived, stretches its paws and yawns, opens one sleepy eye and makes up its mind: I'm going to eat that. I'm going to fill my mouth with it, so that I can barely chew.

"Anything else?" the girl asks, as she pops my Belgian bun onto a plate.

"A hot chocolate please," I say, "with cream and marshmallows."

Then I turn and scan the available seats, deciding on a padded bench right next to the front window. I cross the café, take off my coat and sit and fidget while I wait for the girl to bring it all over to me.

I consider calling my mother to tell her about my self-indulgence. She'd be horrified that I'm out here doing this, rather than vacuuming the stairs and changing the beds, but the waitress arrives, and gives me more important things to attend to.

I go to work on my Belgian bun, picking the icing off. It gunks up under my nails in sticky wodges, and I run them across the ridges of my teeth. I pick a raisin out of the dough and leave it on the side of the plate: don't fancy that one.

There's a large group sitting on the seats in front of the window, two families meeting for coffee by the looks of it. They have three children between them: a baby, a toddler and a preschooler. The women are scraping little chins and mopping up drinks while the men share jokes and laugh.

They all have something to do, I think.

The hot chocolate is finished too fast, and I can't sit here doing nothing. I leave the café and wander along to the amusements. I change fifty pence for a pile of dirty two penny pieces and I study the penny-drops. I stalk them, slyly. Which are most likely to pay out the big money? As I press my last copper in, I curse my luck and surreptitiously knee the machine. It works: two pence is dislodged and I have another shot at winning.

For a while, my luck changes. At one point, I have about two pounds, I reckon. But, of course, I stay until it's all spent, and my knee doesn't work the same trick twice.

There's a little girl in the amusement arcade. I've noticed her on and off, winding her way around the machines, straining to get her hand up into the holes where the money comes out, sitting in the Postman Pat ride-along and pretending it's moving.

She's standing next to me now, looking up at me. She's alone.

"Are you lost?" I reach for her hand, bend down to her height. She nods, and I'm so glad to see this child with her features that are all new to me, her messy orange hair and her dark eyes. "Come on," I smile, "I'll help you – we'll have an adventure finding your mum or dad." I stand and look around.

Now I have something to do, for sure.

"Skye!" a voice barks "Come 'ere!" A large woman with dark hair pulled tightly from her forehead into a tiny, wet topknot strides around the penny-drop machine. She grabs the child's hand from mine, and marches her away without speaking to me. The little girl watches me over her shoulder as they go, like she just had a lucky escape.

I'm thinking of calling Mum when I see, parked outside the amusements, a lonely ice cream van. It's never too cold for an ice cream, so I order a 99 flake. At least it won't melt and dribble down my chin in this weather.

But as I lick it, my eyes focus on the clock tower, and I realise it is half past two. If I don't leave now, I shall be late for school pick up. I have to go. I wolf the ice cream and its spongey cone down, setting off my sensitive molar and reminding me that I must make that dental appointment for Tilda.

I stride back to the car, to discover a ticket slapped onto the windscreen. My parking time expired seven minutes ago while I was licking that bloody ice cream, and the warden is just two cars down from mine.

As I'm tugging the parking ticket out from under the windscreen wiper, my mobile phone goes. I pull it from my pocket.

It's Mum.

ABOUT THE AUTHOR

Liz Jennings grew up in a South London vicarage in the 1970s. She began writing as a student in the 1990s, and her reviews, interviews, features and fiction have appeared in a variety of magazines and publications. Her short stories have won several prizes and her plays have been performed locally in Canterbury, where she lives. Her small group resource, *Short Christians: exploring faith through fiction*, is published by Lioness, and Liz runs story and discussion sessions in church settings. Her website, www.lastminutesmallgroup.com, encourages and equips time-poor small group leaders.

Liz also designs and facilitates creative groups for people with a diagnosis of dementia, and was editor for *Welcome To Our World*, available through the Alzheimer's Society. In 2017 she was awarded the Emma Kent Award for Outstanding Individual Contribution for engaging and empowering people with dementia to enjoy expressing themselves creatively. Her stories are characterised by her use of humour, often bitter-sweet. She is currently working on her second novel.

www.lastminutesmallgroup.com

www.ingramcontent.com/pod-product-compliance
Lightning Source LLC
Chambersburg PA
CBHW020543080526
44583CB00013B/972